Post-Conflict Monuments in Bosnia and Herzegovina

I0461946

At a time of dramatic struggles over monuments around the world, this book examines monuments that have been erected in post-conflict Bosnia and Herzegovina (BiH) since 1996.

Examining the historical precedents for the high rate of monument-building, and its links to ongoing political instability and national animosity, this book identifies the culture of remembrance in BiH as symptomatic of a broader shift: a monumentalisation and privatisation of history. It provides an argument for how to account for the politics of contemporary nation-state formation, control of space, trauma and revisions of history in a region that has been subject to prolonged instability and crisis.

This book will be of interest to scholars in contemporary art, museum studies, war and conflict studies, and European studies.

Uroš Čvoro is Senior Lecturer in Art Theory at UNSW Sydney.

Routledge Focus on Art History and Visual Studies

Post-Conflict Monuments in Bosnia and Herzegovina

Unfinished Histories

Uroš Čvoro

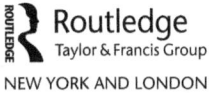
Routledge
Taylor & Francis Group

NEW YORK AND LONDON

First published 2020
by Routledge
52 Vanderbilt Avenue, New York, NY 10017

and by Routledge
2 Park Square, Milton Park, Abingdon, Oxon, OX14 4RN

Routledge is an imprint of the Taylor & Francis Group, an informa business

© 2020 Taylor & Francis

Library of Congress Cataloging-in-Publication Data
Names: Cvoro, Uros, author.
Title: Post-conflict monuments in Bosnia and Herzegovina: unfinished histories/Uroš Čvoro.
Description: New York: Routledge, 2020. | Includes bibliographical references and index.
Identifiers: LCCN 2020005593 (print) | LCCN 2020005594 (ebook) | ISBN 9780367138424 (hardback) | ISBN 9780367138448 (ebook)
Subjects: LCSH: Monuments–Bosnia and Herzegovina. | Nationalism and collective memory–Bosnia and Herzegovina. | Art and history–Bosnia and Herzegovina.
Classification: LCC NB1641.B67 C89 2020 (print) | LCC NB1641.B67 (ebook) | DDC 709.949742–dc23
LC record available at https://lccn.loc.gov/2020005593
LC ebook record available at https://lccn.loc.gov/2020005594

ISBN: 978-0-367-13842-4 (hbk)
ISBN: 978-0-367-13844-8 (ebk)

Typeset in Times New Roman
by Deanta Global Publishing Services, Chennai, India

Za Nanu

Contents

Figures

Acknowledgements

The research and writing of this book were supported by a Faculty Research Grant from UNSW Art & Design in 2018. I would like to thank UDIK, Paul Lowe and Mladen Miljanović. As always, the biggest thank you is to Ena and Marijana.

Introduction

In mid-2017, two media reports captured the complex and politically charged relationship between monuments and the culture of remembrance in Bosnia and Herzegovina (BiH). In March 2017, Sarajevo City Council announced the approval of the construction of a monument near a high school in central Sarajevo to the special forces unit 'Bosnia'. The design of the monument was to feature a group of special forces soldiers celebrating on top of a 'destroyed enemy tank' (Zvanični web portal Općine Centar Sarajevo 2017).[1] A few months later, in June 2017, it was reported that a monument was erected in Petkovci, a village located near the city of Zvornik, dedicated to the fallen local soldiers in the shape of the Serb nationalist three-finger salute (a hand with the thumb, index and middle finger extended) (Aljazeera Balkans 2017). Although the two monuments were conceived to commemorate soldiers from the opposite sides of the 1992–1995 war on BiH, they demonstrated strikingly similar characteristics. Both aimed to establish an ethnically homogeneous and militaristic narrative of sacrifice for the greater good of the nation against an unnamed, yet clearly identifiable, enemy. In the case of the proposed Sarajevo monument, the destroyed tank is associated with Bosnian Serb forces which held Sarajevo under siege; and in the *Petkovci Monument*, the nationalist hand gesture and the proximity of the monument to a site of mass executions of Bosniaks were aimed as a provocation to all non-Serbs. The approach of both monuments to representing 'the other side' was dictated by the ethnic majority population in the local area, and by interest groups connected to the nationalist political elites, which control and approve the construction of monuments (Čusto 2017: 60).

These two monuments encapsulate the throes of monumental obsession and history wars in which BiH appears to be locked for over two decades. Since the end of the 1992–1995 war, over 2100 monuments have been built (Centre for Nonviolent Action 2016; UNDP 2010). At the same time, BiH remains one of the most divided post-conflict societies in the twenty-first century, with ethnic division enshrined in its constitution (Bieber 2002). Its contemporary social and aesthetic complexities around monuments – the high number built, the entrenched nationalism, the systemic denial of genocide and revision of history – resonates with the difficult political situation in the country. More than two decades after the signing of the Dayton Agreement in 1995 that marked the end of war, the country remains mired in the 'ethno-national identitarianism' of its two main constituent entities (the Bosniak-Croat Federation and the Serb-dominated Republika Srpska) and a failed trajectory from violence to reconciliation (Jansen, Brković and Čelebičić 2016). This post-conflict trajectory has been hampered by dispossession of social wealth and infrastructure; a labyrinthine system of government; and routine sequestering of political debate into nationalist rhetoric by the dominant ethnonationalist parties (Mujanović 2013). Consequently, BiH is confronted with the co-existence of three mutually exclusive 'official' narratives that dominate its culture of remembrance, whilst simultaneously disputing each other's claim of ownership over the space and time of the country. In this context, it is difficult to understand BiH monuments as anything other than materialisations of the aggressive nationalist rhetoric that has dominated the country for over two decades (Moll 2013; Sokol 2014; Božić 2017).

   This book takes a sideways look at the nationalism of BiH monuments exemplified by Sarajevo and Petkovci to examine the way in which their interpretation of history – where the past is split between three mutually exclusive versions of national liberation – occurs within the temporal frame of neoliberal global capitalism.[2] I argue that the hyper-production of monuments in BiH after 1996 operates as a monumental free market which validates the neoliberal-nationalist nexus as the sole mode of remembrance and identification. Importantly, in looking beyond the nationalism of BiH monuments, my intention is not to lessen or ignore the impact of the toxic nationalist discourse on the public sphere. Rather, my aim is to look beyond nationalism as the prevailing explanation for the construction of monuments; and I do so by highlighting the connection of nationalism to neoliberalism three decades after the fall of the Berlin Wall, the bloody dissolution of Yugoslavia and the start of post-socialist and post-conflict transition to democracy.

   In one sense, it would be relatively straightforward to articulate the hyper-production of monuments in BiH as a manifestation of the dysfunction of an economically underdeveloped, socially dysfunctional and politically corrupt periphery which still deals with unresolved historical legacies. But this explanation ignores the fact that the very perception of BiH as stuck on the road to Europe accepts a neoliberalist-nationalist nexus as the inevitable and undisputable global order. This book demonstrates how this nexus determines the experience of history and remembrance. On the one hand, my approach includes accounting for the continuing presence of Yugoslav Socialism as a historical reference despite the demonisation of the Yugoslav socialist system as undemocratic, destruction of socialist monuments, and rehabilitation of local World War II Fascists and their collaborators. On the other hand, my approach also includes articulating the relation of monuments to historical revisionism and genocide denial. I argue that historical experience in BiH has been relativised to the point where it functions like predatory capital: it permeates all aspects of the social sphere of everyday life, it relies on corruption and it breeds self-interest. Importantly, in focusing on BiH, my intention is not to argue for its exceptionalism. In fact, one of the key problems of approaching BiH monuments has been the distinct sense of exoticisation from local and international commentators. Rather, I believe that the case of memorial culture in BiH not only reflects the present but anticipates the future of Europe, much like the dissolution of Yugoslavia in the early 1990s anticipated many of the current events in Europe. Furthermore, I also believe that understanding the current memorial culture in BiH beyond the nationalist matrix is key to understanding its connection to neoliberalism. Put differently, I believe that a critique of conservative, religious, patriarchal, nationalist hegemony of the post-Yugoslav societies must also be a critique of the neoliberal capitalist transformation that enabled that transformation.

The Monumental Landscape of BiH

Destruction and construction of monuments accompanies all historical shifts. Repressed histories are uncovered, new heroes and myths are established, older stories are erased or rewritten. BiH has been the ground for major historical events in the last three decades – including the end of state-socialism, the dissolution of Yugoslavia and a bloody destructive war – and these events are reflected in the high number of monuments produced. The majority of existing research on BiH monuments constructed since 1996 argues that they represent the continuation of the 1990s conflict by cultural means[3] (Armakolas 2015; Sheftel 2011). In this sense, BiH monuments have been primarily understood as direct expressions of entrenched nationalism, with three distinct narratives: Bosniak, Croat and Serb.

The emphasis on analysing the nationalism in the monuments is understandable because BiH not only bore the brunt of the Yugoslav wars that resulted in the deaths of over 140,000 people, ethnic cleansing, genocide, displacement of millions of other people and the destruction of a multiethnic country; it also continues to suffer the worst of its devastating consequences. Another key factor contributing to the monumental obsession is that no clear 'winners' emerged out of the conflict (in contrast to Croatia for example), leaving the country with no ethnic majority which could dictate the terms of remembering the past. Peace was established by the Dayton Peace Accord in 1995, which not only enshrined ethnonational division in the constitution of BiH, but also established BiH's geopolitical agency as the meeting point between non-history (enclaved BiH) and history (existence of multicultural BiH in time) (Ćurak 2002: 67). In being an imposition that was removed from historical reality, Dayton marked BiH by 'what it is not': a state of not being a state, made up of three constituent peoples each of which rejects the current BiH as its framework (Bosniaks want a united state; Serbs want independence; Croats want their own enclave). Post-Dayton BiH exists as a product of history that is repressed and denied; in a permanent state of negation.[4] Taking negation as the foundational gesture of contemporary BiH, Chapter 1 will argue that BiH monuments should be understood as three variations of negation: nationalist narratives that ignore and negate victims from the other side; rejection of collectivism; and revisionism of the history of socialism.

What are post-war monuments in BiH? While this book will engage with specific examples, existing surveys of BiH monuments suggest that they include large sculptural monuments, memorial plaques, cemetery memorials, memorial rooms, fountains and squares. My approach and understanding of monuments are guided by this broader understanding of monuments, reflected in the Bosniak-Serbo-Croat word 'spomenik',[5] which includes structures commissioned and erected by a variety of organisations and different levels of political hierarchy, from individuals, to local councils and cantonal authorities. They are located in public squares, parks and streets in cities, village cemeteries, on the side of roads, and remote locations marking specific sites. While there is some range in size from larger memorial centres to smaller markers and structures, stylistically they conform to conservative celebrations of militaristic, masculine and heteronormative nationalism. This can be explained by the fact that most of BiH monuments are designed with little or no input from architects, designers or artists. The absence of involvement from experts gives these monuments a sense of dilettantism and naiveté and justifies writing them off as political weapons with no artistic merit. While this perception has often been repeated in the literature, it overlooks the fact that BiH monuments represent a form of do-it-yourself para-monumentalism with historical precedents in Yugoslavia. While Chapter 2 will discuss these earlier practices, here I want to flag the relation between the present and the socialist monuments in Yugoslavia. The body of monuments constructed after World War II not only form the most significant historical precedent for the current monument construction in BiH, but also remain as the most recognisable form of monumentalism to have emerged out of Yugoslavia.

Socialist Monuments in Yugoslavia

The current proliferation of monuments in BiH marks a continuation of many cultural and political practices from Yugoslavia, including the proximity to political power,[6] and the central place of war in framing the form and content of commemoration.[7] Monuments continue to play central roles in the simultaneous destruction and revision of a shared past and establishment of national histories. As Dubravka Ugrešić argues, the collapse of Yugoslavia in the 1980s and 1990s began with the confiscation of 'Yugoslav collective memory and its replacement by the construct of national memory' (Ugrešić 1996: 34). Changing street names, and removing and destroying monuments, became ways to reframe the past to erase socialism, manipulating the historical trauma of World War II to serve the nationalist agenda. Vjeran Pavlakovic suggests that during the 1990s in Croatia, approximately 3000 monuments, statues and plaques commemorating the partisan movement and anti-fascism were damaged or destroyed (Pavlaković 2013: 903). Others were vandalised or simply left to deteriorate. Robert Burghardt and Gal Kirn use the term 'abandoned monuments' in discussing how historical and political transformations changed these monuments from powerful reminders of an ideologic and collective identity into 'an invisible network of symbolic places, generating an alternative map of the former Yugoslavia' (Burghardt and Kirn 2014: 104). This map includes thousands of sites – of large and small monuments – that spatially document rituals of public memory of socialism in Yugoslavia, as well as their destruction. Contrastingly, attitudes towards monuments across former Yugoslavia during the 1990s reflected the relationship of each political leader to the memory of World War II (Bevan 2006; Bogdanović 1993); while greater numbers of monuments were destroyed in Croatia as part of a historical revisionism tolerated by Franjo Tuđman that 'debased the antifascist resistance and rehabilitated the Ustaša regime' (Pavlaković 2013: 894), the lack of destruction in Serbia reflected Milošević's ethnonationalist politics that absorbed World War II narratives of suffering into the greater mythology of Serbian martyrdom.

But even beyond the local context, Yugoslav monuments have also had increasing global visibility in recent years.[8] This includes fascination and fetishisation of Yugoslav socialist-modernist monuments internationally as evidenced by the scores of publications, documentaries and advertisements, including the 2018–2019 MOMA exhibition about monuments and architecture in Socialist Yugoslavia (Kulić 2018). Yugoslav monuments are being assimilated into post-socialist narratives as ruins (ideological waste), heritage (rebranded as national monuments) or otherworldly aesthetic objects (Herscher 2015). In Chapter 2, I will argue that the socialist monuments from Yugoslavia continue to be an important marker in understanding the post-war monuments in BiH: because there are important continuities in forms of commemoration, and because of the equally important differences to understanding and capturing of historical experience and temporality.

The relationship of monuments to remembering also provides a way to discuss the position of twentieth-century modernism in the present. If the monuments produced during Yugoslavia have become famous because they represent achievements of alternative modernism which was sidelined in 'western discourses', this modernism is still premised on an individualised and heroic sense of authorship. Artists and architects such as Bogdan Bogdanović and Vojin Bakić may be associated with utopian experiments of failed socialism, but the way in which their monumental output is framed is nevertheless reflective of authorial authority. In this sense, while the postwar monuments in BiH demonstrate highly problematic forms of aesthetic and political conservatism, their often-anonymous do-it-yourself production represents a vernacular art form that critiques heroic modernism at the heart of socialist monuments in Yugoslavia. Thus, I am interested in looking at post-war monuments in BiH not to simply dismiss them as aesthetically crude and insensitive representations of nationalism, but rather, to question how, despite their problematic nature, they can tell us something about the complexities of contemporary BiH conditions. Specifically, I am interested in how BiH monuments selectively draw on the symbolic capital of history, and adopt forms of remembering from Yugoslav Socialism, while rejecting or revising that socialism. This interest in the legacy of modernism in the present also relates to my focus on the temporality captured by BiH monuments.

The Temporal Turn

The upsurge of monument construction in BiH in many ways follows the broader process of post-socialist transition. As I have argued previously, a key aspect of this process is not just a revision of history, but also a fundamental shift in conceptions of historical time as evidenced in the temporal turn across humanities in recent years (Čvoro 2018). The turn towards historicising and temporalising the present suggests that the post-1989 end of history and globalisation of time are coming under increased scrutiny. In her work on post-socialism, Susan Buck-Morss positions the temporal schema of transition as 'an expectation' located after the failure of modernity and facing an uncertain present and future (Buck-Morss 2006: 498). In this understanding, transition does not operate as an event with clear temporal boundaries, but rather as a form of 'between time': events unfolding one after another without discernible start or end points.

The proliferation of monuments in BiH should be understood as a response to the change in temporality. While it is clear that they have a nationalist purpose, they can also be seen as attempting to compensate for the loss of historical experience. The war in BiH has, in addition to the physical devastation of life and property, been understood as a rupture in the experience of time, between pre-war 'normality', 'lost time' in war, 'dead time' (Kurtović 2012) or stuck in 'Dayton meantime' (Jansen 2015: 457). Approaching BiH through temporal structures suspended between a known – and often idealised – past of Yugoslavia and a normative, yet unattainable, future of the EU highlights, the extent to which temporal immobility has become as important to the lived experience of BiH as a sense of national identity. This gives new insight into practices of memorialisation in post-conflict contexts, demonstrating that culture and aesthetics of nationalism can lead to monument-building practices that can be read beyond the interpretative key of nationalism.[9] Because BiH is a region that has experienced extreme wartime nationalism and post-war authoritarian populism, there has been a tendency to view all aspects of cultural memory as expressions of entrenched nationalism. Here I am interested in temporality – in particular its relation to the stigmatised legacy of socialism – as a starting point for re-introducing class struggle into the vocabulary of public spaces. It is perhaps one of the key achievements of neoliberalism that the perception of historical experience – and by extension of monuments – in BiH has been almost completely decoupled from class consciousness.

In this sense, my book attempts to move beyond the nationalist focus of the existing scholarship in order to look at temporality as a geopolitical category in BiH monuments.[10] Temporal formations of monuments (discussed in Chapter 3) frame the perception of historical experience and are crucial for the construction of political behaviour. The introduction of this perspective into the existing discussions will deepen our comprehension of how geopolitical time gets normalised through nationalism. It will articulate BiH as a spatio-temporal configuration: a fragmented, supervised, post-war, post-socialist, post-Fordist European periphery, presumed to be on the 'road to Europe' and caught in a perpetual meantime.

Overview of Chapters

The chapters that follow provide the historical, cultural and aesthetic context for the emergence of BiH post-war monuments after 1996, while expanding our understanding of monumental obsession in BiH. Chapter 1 contextualises the monumentalisation of history currently taking place in BiH within the narrative of post-socialist and post-conflict transition. By monumentalisation of history, I am referring to the instrumentalisation of monuments in order to relativise history as open to three nationalist versions: Bosniak, Croat and Serb. Departing from existing research, I shift the focus to examining the post-war monuments as symptomatic of neoliberalism. I then turn towards critiques of nationalism in BiH monuments and examine the tacit assumptions behind their use of counter-monumentality as the term to describe non-nationalist monuments. I argue that these assumptions reflect the general perception of BiH as a transitional post-conflict society on a journey towards democracy. I take a critical approach to this perception because it reduces complex historical processes at a local level to the question of slow progress and development.

Chapter 2 articulates the privatisation of history in post-conflict BiH monuments by looking at continuities and discontinuities between the current state of monuments and practices during and after Yugoslav Socialism. I discuss three forms of built structures that are crucial to understanding the emergence of post-conflict monuments in BiH: socialist monuments from Yugoslavia commemorating World War II anti-fascist Partisan struggle; private 'para-literature' tombstones used by individuals to commemorate their life while denouncing ungrateful families; and illegal and uncontrolled turbo-architecture that emerged in the wake of Yugoslavia's dissolution. While the relation of Socialist Yugoslav monuments to the present is relatively well known, the phenomena of tombstones and turbo-architecture as forms of para-legal built structures have been overlooked as key precedents for understanding the recent monument construction. I argue that they mark important points of change in the understanding of public memorial culture, and the increased role of private ownership of histories and commemorations following the fall of socialism in Yugoslavia.

Chapter 3 outlines the temporal formations of leap, loss, return and delay in BiH monuments. Analysing examples of monuments, it articulates the way in which they relate to the neoliberal teleology from authentic national history to free market. Leap is reflected in monuments that circumvent the 40 years of socialism and the legacy of anti-fascism in BiH (as empty time) and connect the present to the national past in a straight line: manipulation of Narodno Oslobodilačka Borba or NOB (People's Liberation Struggle) and BiH as an anti-fascist political project. Loss is reflected in 'inat' (spite) monuments that politically instrumentalise and weaponise mourning. Return is reflected in monuments that revise histories to establish new national heroes or rewrite known figures in the national key as a way to establish a link to 'authentic' tradition. In contrast to these three narratives that support the neoliberal-nationalist teleology, I argue that the temporal formation of delay includes monuments that reflect alternative approaches. But rather than see this as a nationalist/non-nationalist binary, I argue that delay monuments operate as a distorted mimesis of Western culture and produce a different picture of historical experience.

***

The hyper-production of monuments in a race to commemorate and monumentalise the recent past is not just evident in BiH, but across the region of the former Yugoslavia and beyond. Reports about similar practices in Hungary, Greece, Latvia, the Czech Republic, Slovakia and Macedonia are suggesting a broader trend that is undermining ethical and political principles of open societies. It would be easy to characterise these developments as another example of cultures that are still stuck in the past. But monuments have proved remarkably durable as powerful mobilisers of public and popular sentiments, despite being proclaimed dead decades ago (Huyssen 1995: 254). Recent years have witnessed fierce debates about monuments all over the world – in the US over confederate monuments, and in Australia over the legacy of monuments to colonial figures.

While these events demonstrate the prominent position that monuments continue to occupy in the public imagination, they also highlight the increasing interconnectedness of the far-right and Balkan nationalist mythologies. This was dramatically illustrated in March 2019 during the terrorist attack on two Mosques in Christchurch, which was streamed live online. The shooters' weapons bore the names of figures from Balkan history, all of whom had fought against the Ottoman Empire. Furthermore, the song that was heard playing as the shooter drove to commit the murders glorified Radovan Karadžić (who was in that same week sentenced to life in prison for his role in genocide against Bosniaks). The attack brought Serb nationalism back into the global spotlight and demonstrated the almost mythical status of the Balkans in the collective imagination of the far-right as a place where white Christians have fought against the Muslims for centuries. This blatant manipulation of history, where genocide from the 1990s was framed within the 'clash of the civilisations' narrative, repeated the nationalist message found on many BiH monuments.

These events illustrate the continuing symbolic power of monuments. But as authors have warned previously (Young 1992), the drive to monumetalise the past may also be a drive to forget it. In the present context, we can extend this claim to say that the hyper-production of monuments and the drive to establish new national narratives is underpinned by the desire to forget the fundamental absence of collectivity. Despite political claims about fulfillments of national dreams of independence, there are no winners in BiH after the 1990s, and the first step towards reconciliation may be in making that admission. The second step may be to acknowledge the way in which these claims are determined by retroactively projected national identity politics; Yugoslavia had to end, and BiH had to end up in a bloody conflict. This leads to the view that BiH's last few centuries have been shaped by little more than struggles between national groups for independence and freedom, and that weaponised culture of commemoration is the latest phase of this struggle. This book attempts to suggest that the way forward may be in developing analytical registers to discuss BiH monuments beyond the dominant paradigm of nationalism.

Notes

1 The proposal was rejected by Sarajevo City Council in late 2018, which caused numerous protestations in the media, and a legal challenge by the Sarajevo Veterans Association. While the eventual use of the land remains unclear (as of July 2019), public reactions to the rejection of the proposal confirm my observations about the intention behind the monument. For example, see https://hayat.ba/vijest.php?id=158516 accessed 11 July 2019.

2 As Sandro Mezzadra and Brett Neilson point out, contemporary manifestations of nationalism are adept at accommodating themselves to neoliberal conditions.

> Whether this combination pivots more around economic logics (nurturing protectionist or mercantilist policies), religious identifications, civilizational convictions, or other sources of legitimization, the nation multiplies the heterogeneity that characterizes neoliberalism at the same time that it provides a way to make sense of different neoliberal trajectories and positions within them.
> Mezzadra and Neilson (2019): 51.

3 This also expresses itself in the often-chaotic spatial distribution of monuments. There are several cities, such as Jajce and Brčko, with multiple monuments to different (and opposing) 'victors' and 'liberators'.

4 Post-Dayton BiH has been described as 'negative peace': the post-conflict condition marked by absence of violence, but also marked by absence of key social factors associated with peace such as freedom and justice. Negative peace in BiH means the cessation of violence, but not the removal of triggers which could lead to violence. See Galtung (2009).

5 There are two existing reports that survey post-war monuments in BiH. See UDIK (2017) and Centre for Nonviolent Action (2016). They use a broader notion of 'monument', which reflects the different meaning of the Bosniak-Serbo-Croatian word *spomenik*. Even though the word spomenik literally translates into monument, there has been a tendency in the Anglophone literature to use the word spomenik only when referring to larger structures built during Yugoslavia.

6 A key aspect of the politics of BiH monuments is that their unveiling is used strategically. There are numerous examples of carefully timed opening ceremonies of monuments that are direct provocations to the other side. One example of this is the unveiling of the bust of Momir Talić, the former head of Command in the Army of Republika Srpska, who has been accused of war crimes. The unveiling ceremony took place in Piskavica village near Banja Luka on 10 July 2010. This was one day before the annual commemoration at Srebrenica. The timing is not accidental, nor is the attendance of high-ranking politicians, including Milorad Dodik, who gave speeches praising his contribution to the liberation of Serbs.

7 The first wave of significant monument construction in BiH was in the mid-twentieth century and in relation to the anti-fascist struggle in World War II and the formation of Yugoslavia. While earlier monuments exist – such as monuments to events from World War I – they are few and far between. This is why the BiH monumental landscape can be described as positioned between the foundational monumental mythology of World War II and the 1990s war.

8 In recent years, Yugoslav socialist monuments have appeared in the 2017 edition of the *National Geographic* magazine, 2018 photo-essay in the *Guardian* and exhibitions of private collections such as the FM Centre for Contemporary Art, Milan.

9 My focus on temporality also seeks to address the privileging of space as an analytic category in understanding cultural expressions of nationalism in BiH. For examples that use space as the framework for reading nationalism in BiH, see Ristić 2018; Kulić 2018; Milohnić and Švob-Đokić 2011; Palmberger 2016; Šuber and Karamanić 2012; Beronja and Vervaet 2016; Bjorkdahl and Buckley-Zistel 2016; Stig Sørensen and Viejo Rose 2015.

10 While I approach monuments through the prism of temporality and neoliberalism, it is important to flag other approaches that move beyond nationalism as the interpretative frame in BiH. Recent work includes analysis of the underlying gender logic of nationalism (Helms 2013), 'local' responses to war (Jansen 2002), examination of 'ordinary' and 'everyday' narratives (Kolind 2008; Sorabji 2008) and the role of generational memories in the formation of identities (Palmberger 2016).

References

Armakolas, I. (2015) Imagining Community in Bosnia: Constructing and Reconstructing the Slana Banja Memorial Complex in Tuzla. In Sorensen, M., Stig, L. and Vlejo Rose, D. (eds) *War and Cultural Heritage: Biographies of Place*. New York: Cambridge, pp. 225–250.

Balkans, Aljazeera (2017) Zvornik: Spomenik s tri prsta kod mjesta masovnih egzekucija. Available at: http://balkans.aljazeera.net/vijesti/zvornik-spomenik-s-tri-prsta-kod-mjesta-masovnih-egzekucija (accessed 9 April 2018).

Beronja, Vlad and Vervaet, Stijn (eds) (2016) *Post-Yugoslav Constellations: Archive, Memory, and Trauma in Contemporary Bosnian, Croatian, and Serbian Literature and Culture*. Berlin: Walter de Gruyter GmbH.

Bevan, R. (2006) *The Destruction of Memory: Architecture at War*. London: Reaktion Books.

Bieber, F. (2002) Nationalist Mobilization and Stories of Serb Suffering. *Rethinking History*, 6(1): 95–110.

Bjorkdahl, A. and Buckley-Zistel, S. (eds) (2016) *Spacializing Peace and Conflict: Mapping the Production of Places Sites and Scales of Violence*. London: Palgrave.

Bogdanović, B. (1993) Urbicide. *Space and Society*, 16(62): 8–25.

Božić, G. (2017) Diversity in Ethnicization: War Memory Landscape in Bosnia and Herzegovina. *Memory Studies*, 12(4): 412–432.

Buck-Morss, S. (2006) The Post-Soviet Condition. In IRWIN (ed) *East Art Map*. London: Afterall, pp. 494–499.

Burghardt, R. and Kirn, G. (2014) Hybrid Memorial Architecture and Objects of Revolutionary Aesthetics. In Dunn, A. and MacPhee, J. (eds) *Signal 03*. Oakland: PM Press, pp. 99–131.

Centre for Nonviolent Action (2016) *War of Memories: Places of Suffering and Remembrance of War in Bosnia-Herzegovina*. Sarajevo-Belgrade: Centre for Nonviolent Action.

Ćurak, N. (2002) *Geopolitika Kao Sudbina*. Sarajevo: Fakultet Političkih Nauka.

Čusto, A. (2017) Spomenici i prakse sjećanja u Bosni i Hercegovini. *Zbornik Radova Historijskog Muzeja Bosne I Hercegovine*, 12: 60–69.

Čvoro, U. (2018) *Transitional Aesthetics: Contemporary Art at the Edge of Europe*. London: Bloomsbury.

Galtung, J. (2009) *Mirnim Sredstvima Do Mira*. Beograd: Sluzbeni Glasnik I NVO Jugoistok XXI.

Helms, E. (2013) *Innocence and Victimhood: Gender, Nation, and Women's Activism in Postwar Bosnia-Herzegovina*. Madison: University of Wisconsin Press.

Herscher, A. (2015) From the Politics of Memory to the Memory of Politics: The Socialist Monument in and after Yugoslavia. Paper presented at conference *Memorial For(u)ms –Histories of Possibility*, 3–4 July 2015, Berlin.

Huyssen, A. (1995) *Twilight Memories: Marking Time in a Culture of Amnesia*. New York: Routledge.

Jansen, S. (2002) The Violence of Memories: Local Narratives of the Past after Ethnic Cleansing in Croatia. *Rethinking History*, 6(1): 77–94.

Jansen, S. (2015) *Yearnings in the Meantime: 'Normal Lives' and the State in a Sarajevo Apartment Complex*. New York: Berghahn.

Jansen, S., Brković, Č. and Čelebičić, V. (2016) Introduction: New Ethnographic Perspectives on Mature Dayton Bosnia and Herzegovina. In Jansen, S., Brković, Č. and Čelebičić, V. (eds) *Negotiating Social Relations in Bosnia and Herzegovina: Semiperipheral Entanglements*. Abingdon: Taylor and Francis, pp. 1–28.

Kolind, T. (2008) *Post-War Identification: Everyday Muslim Counterdiscourse in Bosnia Herzegovina*. Aarhus: Aarhus University Press.

Kulić, V. (2018) Orientalizing Socialism: Architecture, Media, and the Representations of Eastern Europe. *Architectural Histories*, 6(1): 1–7.

Kurtović, L. (2012) *Politics of Impasse: Specters of Socialism and the Struggles for the Future in Postwar Bosnia-Herzegovina*. PhD Thesis, University of Berkeley, California.

Mezzadra, Sandro and Neilson, Brett (2019) *The Politics of Operations: Excavating Contemporary Capitalism*. Durham: Duke.

Milohnić, A. and Švob-Đokić, N. (eds) (2011) *Cultural Identity Politics in the (Post)-Transitional Societies*. Zagreb-Ljubljana: IRMO.

Moll, N. (2013) Fragmented Memories in a Fragmented Country: Memory Competition and Political Identity- Building in Today's Bosnia and Herzegovina. *Nationalities Papers*, 41(6): 910–935.

Mujanović, J. (2013) Reclaiming the Political in Bosnia: A Critique of the Legal-Rational Nightmare of Contemporary Bosnian Statehood. *Theory in Action*, 6(2): 109–147.

Palmberger, M. (2016) *How Generations Remember: Conflicting Histories and Shared Memories in Post-War Bosnia and Herzegovina*. London: Palgrave.

Pavlaković, V. (2013) Symbols and the Culture of Memory in Republika Srpska Krajina. *Nationalities Papers: The Journal of Nationalism and Ethnicity*, 41(6): 893–909.

Ristić, M. (2018) *Architecture, Urban Space and War: The Destruction and Reconstruction of Sarajevo*. London: Palgrave Macmillan.

Sheftel, A. (2011) Monument to the International Community, from the Grateful Citizens of Sarajevo: Dark Humour as Counter-Memory in Post-Conflict Bosnia-Herzegovina. *Memory Studies*, 5(2): 145–164.

Sokol, A. (2014) War Monuments: Instruments of Nation-building in Bosnia and Herzegovina. *Croatian Political Science Review*, 51(5): 105–126.

Sorabji, C. (2008) Bosnian Neighbourhoods Revisited: Tolerance, Commitment and Komšiluk in Sarajevo. In Pine, F. and Pina-Cabral, J.D. (eds) *On the Margins of Religion*. New York: Berghahn Books, pp. 97–112.

Stig Sørensen, M.L. and Viejo Rose, D. (eds) (2015) *War and Cultural Heritage: Biographies of Place*. Cambridge: Cambridge University Press.

Šuber, D. and Karamanić, S. (eds) (2012) *Re-tracing Images: Visual Culture After Yugoslavia*. Leiden and Boston: Brill.

UDIK (2017) *The Association for Social Research and Communications Central Register of Monuments*. Sarajevo: UDIK.

Ugrešić, D. (1996) The Confiscation of Memory. *New Left Review*, 218 (July–August): 26–39.

UNDP (2010) *Facing the Past and Access to Justice from a Public Perspective – Special UN Report*. Sarajevo: UNDP.

Young, J.E. (1992) The Counter-Monument: Memory against Itself in Germany Today. *Critical Inquiry*, 18(2): 267–296.

Zvanični web portal Općine Centar Sarajevo (2017) Uručena urbanistička saglasnost za izgradnju spomenika veteranima Odreda policije Bosna. Available at: http://www.centar.ba/novost/12978/urucena-urbanisticka-saglasnost-za-izgradnju-spomenika-veteranima-odreda-policije-bosna (accessed 9 April 2018).

1 Monumentalisation of History

In *The Production of Space*, Henri Lefebvre defines the monument as a singular spatial representation of collective identity (Lefebvre 1991: 220–222). For Lefebvre, monuments attempt to materially transcend time through the appearance of permanence and pathos. They are steeped in the symbolic language of power intended to reflect the political and public memory of the nation-state. By articulating the monumental space as the nexus of materiality and symbolic power, Lefebvre highlights the proximity of the monument to the legitimisation and celebration of the nation-state as a political and a temporal entity. Monuments appear in the aftermath of conflict to commemorate heroes and the fallen, to magnify the glory of the nation and to enable the assimilation of the population into the greater body politic. As Benedict Anderson suggested, monuments have been crucial in establishing the narrative of the nation and the temporal teleology of progress (Anderson 2006: 24–26). In this line of thinking, we can understand the proliferation of monuments in Bosnia and Herzegovina (BiH) as a textbook case of monumentalised nationalism hinged on a militaristic mode of remembering. Monuments are used to mark out ownership of space and territory gained in the war, to immortalise heroes who gave their lives for the greater good of the nation and to create symbols that will repel the enemies of the nation. When travelling through BiH, we can easily identify the ethnic majority in a particular district, town or village; monuments operate like border stones, where they reinforce the existing spatio-temporal division of the country.

Approaching BiH monuments through Lefebvre's framework thus highlights the political, symbolic and material violence that is implicit in the act of monumentalisation:

> To the degree that there are traces of violence and death, negativity and aggressiveness in social practice, the monumental work erases them and replaces them with a tranquil power and certitude which can encompass violence and terror.
>
> (Lefebvre 1991: 222)

We can identify the different forms of violence encompassed through BiH monuments, from the ideological imposition of national identity as the framework through which to remember, through exclusion of remembering and commemorating of 'others', to historical revisionism and destruction of older historical legacies.[1] But, to paraphrase Lefebvre's quote above, if BiH monuments sublimate the violence of nationalism into a representation of certitude, then how do we understand this certitude? What is it?

My departure point in this chapter is that BiH monumentalisation legitimises the certitude of neoliberalism in the guise of nationalism. Historical revisionism and nationalism of BiH monuments are not simply about altering historical facts or about normalising certain forms of remembrance, but also about depoliticisation of history into a contest between different nationalist interpretations. BiH monuments represent a free market which gives the choice from the available nationalist interpretations of history, while this act of interpretation occurs within the unquestioned economic and temporal frame of neoliberalism. BiH monuments seize the past as open to interpretation because history remains as the open space in which to imagine and construct origin myths, while the present historical condition is a question of unreserved integration into global neoliberal capitalism.

Building on my understanding of the nationalist-neoliberal nexus at play in BiH monuments, this chapter contextualises the monumentalisation of history in BiH within the narrative of post-socialist and post-conflict transition. By monumentalisation of history, I am referring to the instrumentalisation of monuments in order to relativise history as only open to three nationalist versions: Bosniak, Croat and Serb.[2] Existing research about BiH monuments has demonstrated the way in which history has been split between three seemingly irreconcilable histories, and the central role of monuments in spatially reinforcing this division. Nationalism in BiH monuments is premised on narratives about struggles for national independence, all of which are framed within the horizon of a transition to neoliberalism. The discourse of nationalism becomes interchangeable with neoliberalism: nationalist discourse about 'sacrifice' and 'pride' normalises the discourse about profit accumulation. And conversely, discourse of economic growth and independence gets conflated with national pride.

In order to cut through this conceptual deadlock in discussions of monuments in BiH, I shift the focus to examining the post-war monuments as symptomatic of neoliberalism. This chapter provides the first step in this process by examining the critical framework that has been used to understand the proliferation of monuments in BiH after 1996. I draw parallels between the way in which the outbreak of war in the former Yugoslavia was interpreted along reductive lines, and the way in which understanding of post-war monuments continues this approach. I then turn towards critiques of nationalism in BiH monuments and examine the tacit assumptions behind their use of counter-monumentality. I argue that these assumptions reflect the general perception of BiH as a transitional post-conflict society on a journey towards democracy.

Neoliberalism in the Guise of Nationalism

I have previously demonstrated the way in which the post-socialist and post-conflict European integration of former Yugoslavia has been supported by the historical revisionism which discredits the existence of Yugoslavia, deeming it a deviation in the history of national development (Čvoro 2018). While an overview of Yugoslavia's history or its dissolution is well beyond the scope here, it is significant to outline the way in which it has been interpreted.

It is generally accepted that Yugoslavia's dissolution was triggered in the early 1980s following the death of Josip Broz Tito. Due to a range of factors – including a global economic recession as well as a lack of political leadership to fill the void left by Tito's cult of personality – the country gradually imploded over the next decade, resulting in war. According to this narrative, from the 1950s to the early 1980s, Yugoslavia was among the countries with the fastest growing economies. The unique socialist system in Yugoslavia, where factories were managed by worker collectives and decision-making was less centralised than in other socialist countries, led to stronger economic growth. While Yugoslavia's growth coincided with a broader growth in European economies, this period ended after the oil price shock in the 1970s. An economic crisis erupted in Yugoslavia, in large part caused by the borrowing of Western capital in order to fund growth through exports (Baten 2016: 64). At the same time, Western economies went into a recession, decreasing demand for Yugoslav imports, creating a large debt problem. The resulting economic downturn led to the bankruptcy of numerous Yugoslav firms in 1989, which was only exacerbated by the adaptation of the International Monetary Fund (IMF) austerity programme in 1990. It led to over 20% of the workforce being unemployed or not receiving wages for months in Serbia, Bosnia and Herzegovina, Macedonia and Kosovo. Real earnings were in a free fall and social programmes collapsed, creating an atmosphere of social despair and hopelessness. This was a critical turning point in the events to follow.

While the collapse of Yugoslavia cannot be explained purely through the IMF-imposed austerity, it played a significant and largely unacknowledged role in the process (Mihaljević 2018). The growing internationalisation of Yugoslavia's economy since the 1970s and increasing dependency on global trade meant that fluctuations of global capital had a more profound impact on Yugoslavia in the 1980s, especially in comparison to other socialist countries (Woodward 1995).[3]

Yet despite this clearly existing link, there has been a general omission of speaking about the role of an emerging global neoliberal capital as a major factor in Yugoslavia's dissolution. As Susan Woodward points out, this failure was due to the pro-market orientation of approaches to the economic problems of socialist (and Western) countries (Woodward 1995: 14). The dominant model of explaining the economic crisis of the 1970s was to claim that stagnation was being caused by the disproportionate influence of unions and unrealistic wage growth. The only solution was to diminish the influence of the unions while deregulating capital; policies that were put in practice by Ronald Reagan in the US and Margaret Thatcher in the UK. This turning point in economic policy marked the birth of neoliberalism as the driving economic and political doctrine (Harvey 2007). The interpretative economic models used to understand the economic crisis not only gave the intellectual support for the rising neoliberalism in Western economies, but also influenced the economic policies of socialist countries. In the case of Yugoslavia, this meant that the only road to recovery from the economic downturn and mass unemployment in the 1980s was austerity: more unemployment, and more opening to the global market.

Approaching Yugoslavia's crisis in the 1980s through the rise of neoliberalism enables us to reframe our understanding of its dissolution and descent into war. In contrast to the predominant models of thinking about the war in Yugoslavia as a result of 'ancient ethnic hatreds' or 'lifting the lid on totalitarianism', we can argue that Yugoslav post-socialist and post-war transition is marked by the emergence of twin narratives of neoliberalism and nationalism, which have imbued the recent past with the imperative of neoliberal democracy within the nation-state as a historical inevitability. In discourses of transition, the nation-state is deployed as the frame within which to rewrite history, establish clear ethnic majorities and marginalised minorities, and demarcate territorial sovereignty.

What does it mean to deploy the nation-state as the temporal frame in the context of BiH monuments? It means to acknowledge the synergy between the formation of post-Yugoslav nation-states and an aggressive shift into neoliberalism. The wars of the 1990s can be understood as the first (most primitive and aggressive) form of resource accumulation through land grab.[4] This is followed by the stripping of social assets through privatisation, de-industrialisation and demolition of the social safety support. This process of fast and aggressive post-conflict privatisation has been described by Naomi Klein as 'shock doctrine' capitalism (Klein 2007), which operates in BiH as a series of negations.

Regarding monuments, on the one hand this negation involves the systematic destruction of the history of Yugoslavia and anti-fascism: the destruction of World War II partisan monuments (such as the ruination and vandalism of Bogdan Bogdanović's landmark Partisan Cemetery in Mostar); the appropriation of World War II partisan legacies into nationalist narratives (such as the Serbification of commemoration of fallen World War II partisan fighters at the Kozara monument, or the removal of a Partisan monument in Bileća to make room for a statue of Draža Mihailović); and revision of histories (such as the erection of a monument to 'victims of partisans' near Široki Brijeg).

All these processes point to a systemic attempt to distance the present regimes from socialism, while colonising the legacy of the World War II anti-fascist struggle into nationalist narratives of suffering and victimhood (Begić and Mraović 2014; Mills 2012; Ćusto 2013).

On the other hand, this negation also involves the celebration of ethnocentric national history, while denying or repressing others. This is where the three versions of history in BiH (Serb, Croat and Bosniak) demonstrate consistency in how they are constructed. Monuments from all three sides connect four key historical periods: the end of the nineteenth century, including the collapsing Ottoman and Habsburg empires; World Wars I and II; and the 1990s war. One way of understanding this historical montage is that it connects nineteenth-century romanticist narratives of martyrdom, empires and glory to twentieth-century narratives of the struggle for national recognition against communist totalitarianism, which culminate in the 1990s conflict as the ultimate struggle for national independence. Two examples that illustrate this montage-based approach to history are a Serb monument near Modriča which commemorates a battle from 1858, World War II Četnik units and Serbs fallen in a 1992 battle; and a Croat monument in Dračevo near Čapljina which commemorates fighters from the 1990s and an 1875 uprising against 'Turkish and Serb oppression on Croat land'.[5]

But another way of understanding the prevalence of the timelines established by BiH monuments is one of continuity between the present nationalist regimes and their historical counterparts which were either subservient to nineteenth-century European imperialism or acted in its interests. These monuments show colonial expansion, or vassal ruler land grab (both primitive forms of capital accumulation) *in the guise of struggles for national pride and independence*. National homogeneity – the obsession with constructing 'our' history – ignores the way in which economic exploitation and dispossession were intrinsic to the narrative of national awakening. Put differently, what BiH monuments do not mention is that the dead peasant-soldiers that fought in 'historical' uprisings were fighting in the interests of wealthy land owners. Equally, the imperative to establish a historical through-line to the national liberation ignores that this national liberation has been fulfilled through economic and social devastation. BiH monumental nationalism is thus an acceptance of global capitalism as the framework within which to construct national myths. In championing nationalism as the sole mode of identification and remembering, it obscures the process of 'economic dispossession by a class of criminal-political elites' (Mujanović 2014: 141).

The Neoliberal Triptych

This synergy between nationalist monuments and neoliberalism in BiH was vividly illustrated on my visit to the monument to the fallen Croat soldiers in the Modran village in late 2018.

Built in 2007, *Monument to the Fallen from Modran Village and Surrounding Areas* is located on a periphery of a small village near Derventa, most of which still remains destroyed. Burnt out and devastated houses with visible bullet holes dot the muddy unkept road that leads through the village. The few houses that have been rebuilt show very few signs of life. In a small cemetery on the outskirts of this village is a monument to 'fallen Croat soldiers' from the local area in the 1940s. The monument bears the coat of arms of the Derventa HVO (*Hrvatsko Vijeće Obrane* or Croatian Defence Council) as the official military organisation authorising and financing the monument, and a passage from the Bible inscribed in the centre of the structure.

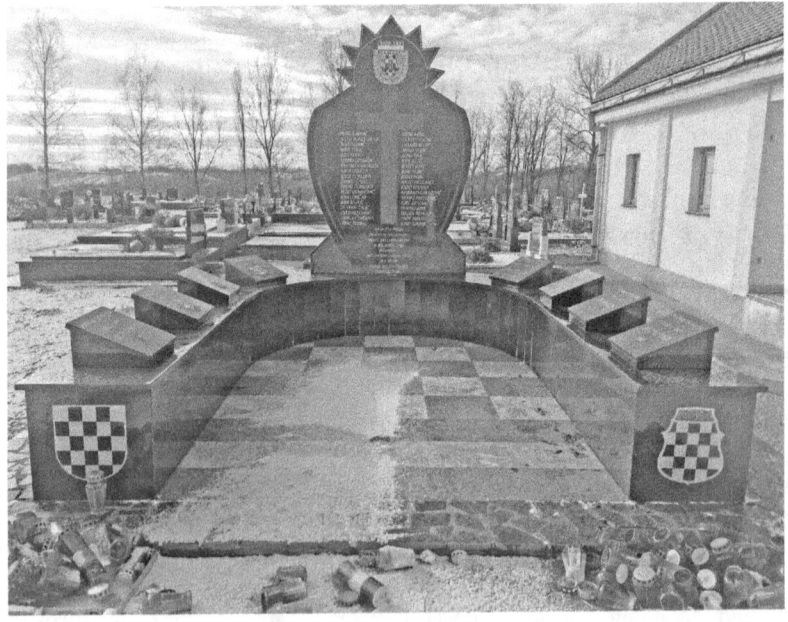

Figure 1.1 Derventa, *Monument to the Fallen from Modran Village and Surrounding Areas* (Derventa Spomenik poginulima sela Modran i okolnih mjesta).

It establishes a symbolic link between the 1990s and the puppet-Fascist Croat State NDH from the 1940s: the entire monument is shaped like the letter 'U' (the symbol of Ustaše) with the Croat checkers in the centre (the corner checker is white, which was the symbol of Ustaše).

Less than 10 kilometres away from the Modran village is the Gajić Motel in Šešlije. Located on a major crossroad on the road from Derventa to Doboj, the gimmicky castle towers and the garish pink-green of this two-storey road-house hotel and mini shopping centre are a reminder of the first wave of post-conflict 'reconstruction' of BiH.[6]

On the day I visited the motel, the clientele consisted of locals drinking coffee (and discussing plans on how to leave BiH) and a busload of people on their way to temporary work in Slovenia and the Netherlands. Gajić Motel is on a crossroad of a road that is increasingly less used due to the '9th of January' highway between Doboj and Banja Luka, whose entrance is nearby. Named after the 'Day of Republika Srpska' (the date of the declaration of the independence of that entity in 1992) – which is contested in the Federation as unconstitutional – the highway was opened in late 2018 as the result of cooperation between the government of Republika Srpska and an international company.[7] On the day of my trip, I was struck by how the highway

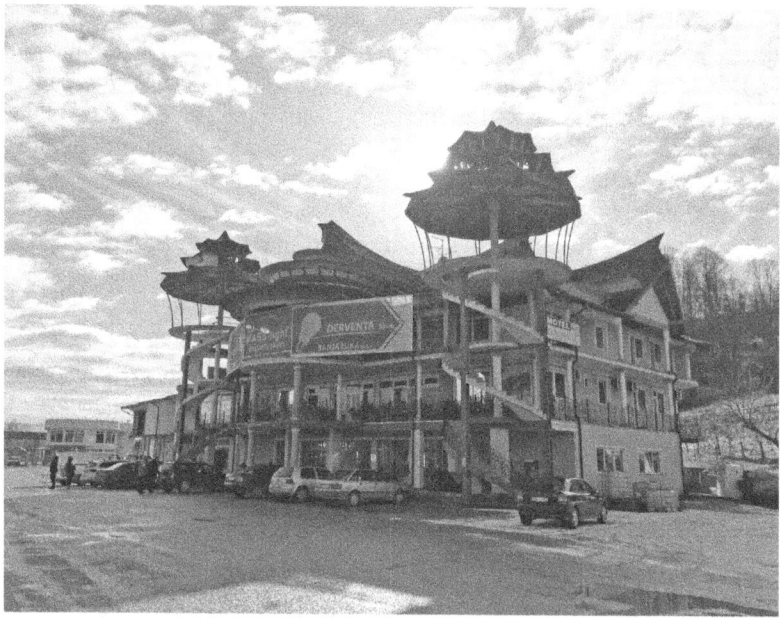

Figure 1.2 Gajić Motel Šešlije.

was almost as deserted as the Modran Village monument. Built as a major infrastructural project intended to reduce travel time between the economic hubs in Republika Srpska, there was minimal traffic on the highway because the toll is so excessively high that most citizens cannot afford to use it.

There are two ways to read this constellation of monument-motel-highway: through the ethnonational focus, and as neoliberal infrastructure in the guise of nationalism.

If viewed through the ethnocentric lens, our departure point would be to point out that a Croat monument was constructed in a Croat-majority village on the territory of the Serb-majority Republika Srpska entity in BiH. While the monument can be seen as reflective of the freedom by the local community to express its identity by commemorating its heroes, it nevertheless takes place in the context of a territory that is governed by the Serb political majority. This is confirmed by its remote location: the monument is part of a cemetery on the outskirts of a deserted village, which is in turn remote from major roads. In other words, it is largely invisible to anyone except for the local community. Nearby to this village is a motel owned by a local high-ranking Serb police officer built on an important crossroad during the post-conflict reconstruction. The motel was built to maximise on the increased traffic which connects the regional centres in the newly established Republika Srpska. The motel is located near the entrance to the highway constructed to better connect these regional centres and celebrate the post-conflict economic prosperity of the Serb-dominated entity. The economic success of Republika Srpska is highlighted in the name of the highway (January 9) and a banner prominently displayed on an overpass on the highway featuring the leading Serb politician Milorad Dodik and Serbian president Aleksandar Vučić, which celebrates their friendship. Furthermore, the name of the highway is a gesture of defiance of the Bosniak-dominated BiH Federation, which is constantly seeking to undermine the independence and self-governance of Republika Srpska. The construction of the highway is an important first step in the strengthening of cultural and historical links between Serbs in Bosnia and Serbia, and a gesture signalling the desire of the Serb population to seek independence from BiH, and eventual unification with Serbia into one state. The completion of this highway on the eve of the 2018 BiH federal elections is a timely reminder of the effectiveness and impact of the leadership of Dodik and his party, which was validated by the electoral win of the SNSD in Republika Srpska.

The problem with this account is that it not only disguises economic exploitation under the rhetoric of national independence and pride, but it also disguises the state interventionism in Republika Srpska under the auspice of national security and interest. While the January 9 highway opened as an expression of the supportive state apparatus, another series of events were reaching their culmination, and showing another side of Republika Srpska. Throughout 2018, Banja Luka was witnessing massive public protests over the unexplained circumstances of the death of David Dragičević on 18 March 2018. What started as protests by his father demanding answers over the unexplained circumstances over the young man's death grew into a mass movement called 'justice for David', which took on transnational solidarity by linking with 'justice for Dženan' protests against the unexplained circumstances of the 2016 death of a young Bosniak Dženan Memić in Sarajevo. The protests across BiH were directed at state power and corruption, not based on ethnic or religious differences, but on the control of information and power. After public gatherings were banned by authorities in Banja Luka, resulting in a number of arrests in December 2018, David's father relocated to Vienna, effectively taking the movement with him. Repeating the mass migration of people from BiH, the fight for justice transformed into diasporic protests in the EU. David's body was re-buried in Vienna, his parents relocated to Vienna and the movement continues to demand justice from Vienna. The migration of the protests has been interpreted by the public as a defeat of an attempt to question the police-state apparatus by the Serbs in a Serb-dominated entity. These events illustrate the way in which 'national' leadership of Republika Srpska is showing all the signs of the withering away of the neoliberal state, except in cases of security, where the state-police apparatus became highly visible.

Bearing in mind the visible-invisible state mechanism as the backbone of neoliberalism, the second approach to the monument-motel-highway constellation is to think about them as an infrastructural triptych of neoliberalism. In other words, I approach them as temporal markers of moments in the neoliberal history of BiH: as a cultural and economic infrastructure reflecting transition. Seen in this context, there is a palpable sense of atavistic desperation about the nationalist monument in Modran. Rather than a sign of territorial ownership or aggressive nationalism, the monument resembles a symbol of a war that was always lost. Built in a Croat majority village and dedicated to Croats by Croats – albeit on the territory of Republika Srpska – it marked the land that has been since abandoned by all except those who were unable to leave. In this sense, the Modran monument embodies the first stage of the neoliberalisation of BiH: landgrab as the first phase of capital accumulation. Gajić Motel represents the second phase: the lawlessness of post-conflict privatisation through shady deals by figures with political connections. The highway is the third phase: large-scale privatisation financed by cooperation between government and foreign investment.

The way in which meaning moves through and between the material and symbolic space between the three constructions captures the different phases of BiH's descent into global neoliberalism. They close the loop of exploitation, privatisation and inequality in being constructions enabled by the state largely devoid of life and designed to speed up the movement of people out of the country. In this context, nationalism symbolised by the Modran monument has the appearance of a first step towards a predefined future: functional rather than pathological. The nationalism that in many ways initiated the process of transition to neoliberalism that has not only since overtaken it but incorporated its pathology. BiH appears as a state shifting from allowing expressions of monumental fascism, to allowing illegal motel construction, and finally to collaborating with global capital to build large-scale infrastructure.

The full meaning of the Modran Village monument can only be grasped in the montage with the motel and the highway. Contrasted against the archaic language of the nationalist monuments and the intentionally attention-grabbing architectural pastiche of the motel is the silent symbolic, political and economic 'language of infrastructure' (Franke 2005: 7) symbolised by the new highway. Infrastructure here not only defines the privilege of movement, but also defines the flow of physical and temporal space between the 'promise' of EU and 'Balkan' periphery. Caught in the post-Dayton, meantime – a temporal suspension between a war that has not quite ended and a future that has not yet been embarked upon (Jansen 2015) – the only option for BiH returning to 'normality' is the integration into global circuits of capital, under the auspice of national sovereignty. This was illustrated by one of the overpasses of the highway that featured a large banner with the phrase 'Light at the end of the tunnel' and photographs of Serbia's president Aleksandar Vučić and Bosnian Serb politicial leader Milorad Dodik on either side of the slogan.[8] Seemingly, political propaganda was accurate for once, even if this was not its intention. Rather than a guarantee of a certain bright future of all Serbs, moving towards national independence and unification under the watchful eye of their populist authoritarian leaders Vučić and Dodik, the light at the end of the tunnel is quite literally *more highway*; more infrastructure designed to attract and benefit global capital. The neoliberal triptych of monument-motel-highway powerfully captures the directionality of 'Balkan nationalism' in the process of 'becoming Europe' by being integrated, or dissolved, into the invisible global infrastructure of capitalist production. Staunch nationalists seamlessly flow and transform into the global precarious migrant workforce necessary to fuel and sustain neoliberalism.

While the Modran monument-hotel-highway triptych is a striking example of the way in which nationalist normativity gets incorporated into neoliberal infrastructure, there are numerous others to be found across BiH. Pavle Levi's analysis of the Omarska camp site – which I will return to in Chapter 3 – provides powerful insight into the process of transforming and commercialising a site of nationalist violence: from ethnic cleansing, through a nationalist movie set, to a foreign owned extraction mine (Levi 2009). This nexus between physical or symbolic nationalist violence and private capital is used to build neoliberal infrastructure in a recurring theme in BiH monuments. In July 2019, the City of Banja Luka announced a public competition for proposals to develop a pedestrian zone, which will complement the existing and planned commercial and historical buildings (City of Banja Luka 2019). The competition requires the planning of location and concepts for two monuments: one to mark the integration of Republika Srpska into 'Yugoslav space' which marked the affirmation of the centuries-old tendency of the Serbs towards independence; and a second one to commemorate the fallen fighters of the 'Defensive-homeland war 1992–1995'.[9] The competition stipulates that the proposed monuments are to celebrate Serb nationalism, which is to be incorporated into the commercial interests of the site.

Another striking feature of the monument-hotel-highway triptych is the contrast between poorly built and unkept nationalist constructions, and neoliberal infrastructure. This creates a two-tier system between the monuments whose poor crumbling state gives them the appearance of ruins in a matter of years after construction, and the cutting-edge expensive infrastructure. Both are financed by private capital, but the difference of quality and durability creates a powerful temporal effect. Monuments have the appearance of what Frederic Jameson calls nostalgia for the present (Jameson 1992); instant ruin aesthetics that create a sense of longing for lost nationalist pride, which is simultaneously monumentalised and mourned for as lost. As a result, BiH monuments look like short-term constructions, designed to achieve a shock effect, and likely to be replaced during the next electoral cycle.[10] By contrast, neoliberal infrastructure conjures up images of a ruthless exclusionary future: shopping centres, expensive apartment blocks, high-speed highways and foreign-owned hydroelectric plants, designed to enable the extractive predatory capital in BiH (Arsenijević 2019).

If nationalist monuments such as the example in Modran Village symbolically accept and enable neoliberalism as the temporal frame within which to revise the past, what is perhaps more striking is how the critical response to BiH monuments also accepts the transition to neoliberalism as the unquestioned framework. In the next section, I will show how in their overwhelming focus on the nationalism, existing critiques of BiH monuments fail to question neoliberalism as the presumed answer to nationalism. This is evident in the over-reliance on the term counter-monument as a shorthand for the examples of non-nationalist approaches to monuments in BiH. By questioning the tacit assumptions behind using counter-monumentality as the alternative to nationalist monuments, I argue that counter-monumentality also binds these critiques to the temporal horizon of transition. Namely, in its emphasis on consensus and (western) democracy as the desired outcomes of the process of remembrance, counter-monumentality is premised on the ideology of transition.

The Monument and the Counter-monument in BiH

Counter-monumentality is a term that was developed by historian James E. Young to capture the proliferation of non-traditional approaches to monuments in Germany and the US since the 1980s (Young 1992, 1994, 2000, 2010). Articulated by Young in his discussion of an emerging trend in 1980s Germany dealing with the history of the Holocaust, counter-monuments are described as 'brazen, painfully self-conscious memorial spaces conceived to challenge the very premises of their being' (Young 1992: 271). Young's paradigmatic example of counter-monumentality, Jochen Gerz and Esther Shalev-Gerz's *Monument against Fascism, War and Violence* (1986) in Harburg, featured a 12m-high column which was open to the public to make inscriptions on its surface. The work was lowered into the ground over the course of several years, meaning that the inscriptions gradually disappeared. Following the final lowering in 1993, the column disappeared, returning the burden of remembering (of the object as well as the debates) to the public. Contrary to the artists' expectations, the inscriptions often featured funny drawings, graffiti and offensive symbols (including swastikas), which Young interpreted as reflective of the complexity of public sentiments towards the past, and illustrative of the possibilities and limitations of monuments as 'counterindexes' of time, memory and history (Young 1992: 273). More broadly, Young argued, *Monument against Fascism* demonstrated the way counter-monuments use negative, invisible and disappearing forms to critique monolithic and triumphalist conceptions of the past through open and fragmented memory. Since the publication of Young's analysis in 1992, the term counter-monumentality has been taken up in a range of theoretical discourses and artistic practices as a critical tool for re-evaluating the relationship of public art to changing political systems (Stevens, Franck and Fazakerley 2012: 952).

Young's work emerged in the context of intense public debate in Germany regarding public commemoration, the function of didactic monuments and the role of memory in negotiating the implications of the past. While it has endured as an influential concept in studies of monuments and collective remembrance, more recent scholarship has pointed out a number of limitations in counter-monumental theory: the way in which counter-monuments' claim to a unique status reproduces a new (albeit different) discourse of monumentality (Lupu 2003); how the deployment of the discourse of counter-monuments in diverse contexts has become gender normative (Thakkar 2009) and proximate to male-German post-war identity (Tomberger 2010: 231); how counter-monumentality sustains problematic assumptions such as the equation of monuments with fascism and conflation of the monument with personal memory (Crownshaw 2008); and how counter-monumentality trades difference and disagreement for consensus in the experience of the audience (Tello 2016: 20).

The discourse of counter-monument is invoked in nearly all available accounts of post-war monuments in BiH and is applied with little or no consideration for the context from which the term emerged, or the translatability of the term. The uncritical use of counter-monumentality in thinking about monuments in BiH is reflected in the wide and contradictory range of meanings it invokes: monuments that refute the prevailing ethnonational narratives by focusing on popular culture figures such as the Bruce Lee statue in Mostar (Ristić 2018: 19–21; Bolton and Muzurović 2010: 195); monuments that critique the existing culture of rememberance through everyday objects such as the can of spam in Nebojša Šaric Šoba's *Monument to the International Community, from the Grateful Citizens of Sarajevo* (Sokol 2014: 120; Sheftel 2011: 158); the archival work of *The Association of Women Victims of War* organisation to document traumatic rape memory from Srebrenica (Jacobs 2017: 432); to nationalist monuments that exist only to provoke the other side (Boerhout and van Driel 2012: 216; Sokol 2014: 116).

The wholesale use of Young's conception in discussions of BiH monuments can be interpreted as reflecting a more general confusion over a term which was describing a body of work in a specific historical context that does not translate across cultural, historical and political borders (Stevens, Franck and Fazakerley 2012: 952). Young suggested in 1999 that 'the concept of the counter-monument in Germany, has begun to constitute something akin to a "national form"' (Young 1999). In other words, we can read this conceptual misunderstanding as a signal that the use of counter-monumentality to read monuments in BiH is not productive and not applicable since the historical and aesthetic reference points in BiH after 1996 are vastly different to those in 1980s Germany. Despite the frequent appearance of the term counter-monument in the literature, the meaning of the term remains vague and is 'often used interchangeably with other terms that may have very different connotations, including anti-monument, non-monument, negative-form, deconstructive, non-traditional and counter-hegemonic monument' (Stevens, Franck and Fazakerley 2012: 952).

Here I want to argue that this confusion is symptomatic of the broader issues underpinning the existing approaches to the post-war monuments in BiH. These discussions import understandings of commemoration, history and monuments into the local context in a way that mirrors the broader perception of BiH as an encounter of history and non-history. This is evident in one of the key assumptions in the application of counter-monuments on post-war BiH monuments: the conflation of monuments with totalitarianism.

Young's departure point for his discussion of counter-monuments were the traditional figurative monuments made of enduring materials like marble, granite or bronze, which were intended to symbolically dominate the physical site and perform specific didactic functions. Numerous authors have critiqued this notion of the monument, from its grandiose aspirations to immortality (Choay 2001: 7), its triumphalism (Danto 1987: 112; Sturken 1998: 274), ideologically problematic commemorations of 'great' histories and men (Janson 1976: 1), to uncritical 'age- value' (Riegl 1982: 21).

But Young's analysis not only assumed the traditional monument as its departure point, his analysis emerged at a specific historical juncture, which associated monumentality with particular ideologies. Young's analysis was written in the context of 1989 'end of history' (Fukuyama 1989), which announced the turn from oppositional Cold War politics and the end of grand ideological narratives. Young's account relies on the 'two totalitarianisms' narrative for understanding monuments and modernism in Europe. Against the history of modernist avant-garde rejection of the monuments, Young describes the monuments' 'consort' with two of the twentieth century's most egregiously totalitarian regimes: Nazi Germany and Soviet Union's revival of monumentality (Young 2000: 96–97). This is crucial to his understanding of the historical and ideological baggage of monuments.

Young's point about monuments as the symbolic support for totalitarianism needs to be understood in relation to the broader narrative of post-1989 'normalization' of history, in which former Eastern Bloc societies were seen as returning to a 'zero point' before the history of capitalist growth (supported by the development of the nation-state) was disrupted by disastrous, totalitarian socialist episodes. The wholesale engineering of the past across Europe was perfectly epitomised in the resolution passed by the EU Parliament on 2 April 2009 on 'European conscience and totalitarianism' (EU Parliament). This resolution announced Europe as historically liberated from two totalitarianisms – fascism and communism – as a way of securing the path to democracy in the twenty-first century. While it is undeniable that communism produced suffering and deaths under dictatorships such as Stalin's Russia, EU Parliament resolution placed communism and fascism on the same totalitarian plane and established the present as a post-ideological and post-historical platform from which the past can be relativised.

Part of this relativisation is in subsuming the expressive abstract forms of World War II monuments in former Yugoslavia – reminiscent of their international contemporaries yet ignored by the Western art historical canon until very recently – under the narrative of Cold War modernism. The increased global visibility of Yugoslav memorials – in publications, music videos, movies and social networks – is inscribed into the Cold War ideological framework that reduced all agency under state socialism to totalitarian control that sees monuments as 'lost', 'otherworldly' or 'vanishing' material remnants of that totalitarianism (Horvatinčić 2012; Kulić 2018).

Using counter-monumentality as an interpretive framework for understanding BiH monuments concedes that the monumentalisation of history in BiH is final and irreversible. This concession shapes the terms of the debate and the way in which monuments are apprehended, with two important consequences.

First, it positions nationalism as the inevitable outcome of socialism. It views Yugoslavia as a totalitarian prison that had to end in bloodshed; it views the history of BiH as the most multicultural part of Yugoslavia as a centuries-old struggle for national independence of its three main ethnic groups; and it views post-war monuments as material and symbolic reflections of this historical determinism. This understanding of history positions the World War II Yugoslav monuments as a depoliticised historical difference that is available for historical revision and relativisation insofar as they need to reflect the historical truths useful to the nationalist present. As the next chapter will argue, socialist monuments are not the site of historical difference but a continuing presence in current forms of commemoration. This is evidenced in important continuities and discontinuities between the present time and forms of commemoration in Socialist Yugoslavia, which presents critical openings for understanding the present beyond the nationalist paradigm.

Second, the two totalitarianisms narrative inherent in the notion of counter-monumentality accepts neoliberalism as the solution to the nationalism in BiH, rather than its cause. Counter-monumentality emerges in the post-1989 moment of transition to neoliberalism and reflects its understanding of the former Eastern Bloc as sites of totalitarianism that needs to be left behind. The neoliberal narrative of transition from centralised economies, totalitarianism and conflict towards deregulated markets, stability and European democracy reflects BiH through the prism of belated modernisation. In her analysis of political discourses concerning the accession of the former Yugoslav countries to the EU, Tanja Petrović shows how the narrative of EU integration in the Balkans is presented as the only way for former Yugoslav societies to unburden themselves from historical baggage, from nationalism and other twentieth-century anchors, and join the future-oriented international community (Petrović 2012: 10). However, as Petrović argues, rather than providing an alternative to nationalism(s), transition and EU integration have produced new forms of nationalism. In remaining blind to the nationalist-neoliberal nexus at play in these new forms, the idea of counter-monumentality obfuscates a critical assessment of historical accountability and responsibility. It simplifies complex and ongoing cultural processes that have contributed to the present in BiH and relegates them to the status of less important discourses.[11] Chapter 2 will discuss these processes.

Understanding the conceptual consequences of using counter-monumentality in the context of BiH monuments is significant if we are to try to untangle the nationalist-neoliberal nexus. It includes understanding that the ultimate aim of the nationalist machine in BiH is not to resolve the 'national question', but to create new national problems in order to reproduce itself within the horizon of neoliberalism. It also includes understanding that approaching BiH monuments only as part of this national question is an acceptance of nationalist-neoliberalism as the sole mode of identification and remembering.

Notes

1   W. J. T. Mitchell also talks about forms of violence in public art, making a distinction between '(1) the image as an act or object of violence, itself doing violence to beholders, or "suffering" violence as the target of vandalism, disfigurement, or demolition; (2) the image as a weapon of violence, a device for attack, coercion, incitement, or more subtle "dislocations" of public spaces; (3) the image as a representation of violence, whether a realistic imitation of a violent act, or a monument, trophy, memorial, or other trace of past violence' (Mitchell 1992: 37–38).
2   This relativisation of history is vividly illustrated in the town of Brčko, where three monuments celebrating the fallen fighters from each side exist in close proximity to each other, located within the town centre. It is important to note that monuments are only one form of relativisation of history. A similar process is also taking place in primary and secondary education, which is being pathologically segregated along 'national' lines.
3   Woodward's study was based on research carried out during the 1980s, and intended to counteract the journalistic and popular fascination with nationalism as the cause of war. By the time Woodward's book was published in 1995, the country had already fallen apart, and the book became an alternative history of Yugoslavia's demise, often sidelined in the scholarship on Yugoslavia. The re-discovery of Woodward's work in recent years is itself symptomatic of the increased interest in thinking about Yugoslavia differently.
4   In recent years, there has been a recognition of war and ethnic cleansing (as well as post-war economics) in BiH through the Marxist notion of accumulation by dispossession. Marx describes the origins of bourgeoisie capitalism via a process of primitive or original accumulation. This includes the colonial conquest, dispossession and enslavement in America and Africa, as well as the commercial war of European colonisers. For example, see Mujanović (2014).
5   There are many other examples that illustrate these kinds of historical narratives. For an overview of BiH monnuments along 'national lines' including a statistical analysis, see UDIK 2018.
6   I will discuss the motel in more detail in the next chapter.
7   This is one of a number of large infrastructural projects by international conglomerates currently under way in the region. In many cases, such as the construction of the Pelješac Bridge by the Croatian government in partnership with a Chinese construction frim, these projects breach the sovereignty of BiH.
8   The same banner was placed on a highway in Southern Serbia. Both banners were removed in October 2019 by members of political opposition parties.
9   The full documentation of the competition including the specifications of the planned monuments are available at the City of Banja Luka website www.banjaluka.rs.ba/konkurs-centralna-gradska-zona/ accessed 23 July 2019.

10 During my field research, when I asked the locals about the poor state of monuments so soon after their completion, the answer I heard most often was 'that is fine, we will just build another one'.

11 Here I am drawing on Boris Buden's idea of 'vernacularisation'; the shifting of local experience and history as less important historical baggage against the domination of English as the cultural and conceptual lingua franca:

> re-vernacularization ... is a retrograde process in which a distinctive and fully formed national and cultural language falls back into the condition of a vernacular from which it had raised itself since the sixteenth century ... in Europe and elsewhere, we are witnessing today the emergence of a new cultural and linguistic condition that might be described as a sort of 'a neo-medieval diglossia – high: English/low: other languages'.

(Buden 2019: 145)

References

Anderson, B. (2006) *Imagined Communities: Reflections on the Origin and Spread of Nationalism*, rev. ed. London: Verso.

Arsenijević, A. (2019) "The Proletarian Lung": The Struggle for the Commons as Memory Politics in Bosnia and Herzegovina. *Springerin* (1). Available at: https ://www.springerin.at/en/2019/1/die-proletarische-lunge/ (accessed 23 July 2019).

Baten, J. (2016) *A History of the Global Economy. From 1500 to the Present.* Cambridge: Cambridge University Press.

Begić, S. and Mraović, B. (2014) Forsaken Monuments and Social Change: The Function of Socialist Monuments in the Post-Yugoslav Space. In Moeschberger, S.L. and DeZalia, R.A.P. (eds) *Symbols that Bind, Symbols that Divide.* London: Springer, pp. 13–37.

Boerhout, L. and van Driel, B. (2012) Memory Walk: An Interaction- Oriented Project to Interrogate Contested Histories. *Intercultural Education*, 24(3): 211–221.

Bolton, G. and Muzurović, N. (2010) Globalizing Memory in a Divided City: Bruce Lee in Mostar. In Conrad, Sebastian and Assmann, Aleida (eds) *Memory in a Global Age: Discourses, Practices and Trajectories.* London: Palgrave Macmillan, pp. 181–198.

Buden, B. (2019) It's Getting Darker Around the Central Sun of Freedom: *Capital, Translation and the Re-feudalization of Capitalism.* In Osborne, Peter, Alliez, Eric and Russel, Eric-John (eds) *Capitalism: Concept, Idea, Image Aspects of Marx's Capital Today.* London: CRPEM Books, pp. 135–163.

Choay, F. (2001) *The Invention of the Historic Monument.* Cambridge: Cambridge Press University.

City of Banja Luka (2019) Available at: http://www.banjaluka.rs.ba/konkurs-centr alna-gradska-zona/ (accessed 23 July 2019).

Crownshaw, R. (2008) The German Countermonument: Conceptual Indeterminacies and the Retheorisation of the Arts of Vicarious Memory. *Forum for Modern Language Studies*, 44(2): 214–223.

Čusto, A. (2013) *Uloga spomenika u Sarajevu u izgradnji kolektivnog sjećanja na period 1941–1945. i 1992–1995. – komparativna analiza.* Sarajevo: Institut za istoriju.

Čvoro, U. (2018) *Transitional Aesthetics: Contemporary Art at the Edge of Europe.* London: Bloomsbury.

Danto, A. (1987) *The State of the Art.* New York: Prentice Hall Press.

EU Parliament. Available at: http://www.europarl.europa.eu/sides/getDoc.do?pubR ef=-//EP//TEXT+TA+P6-TA-2009-0213+0+DOC+XML+V0//EN (accessed 13 May 2016).

Franke, A. (2005) *B-Zone: Becoming Europe and Beyond.* Actar: Barcelona.

Fukuyama, F. (1989) The End of History? *The National Interest*, (16): 3–18.

Harvey, D. (2007) *A Brief History of Neoliberalism.* Oxford: Oxford University Press.

Horvatinčić, S. (2012) The Peculiar Case of *Spomeniks*: Monumental Commemorative Sculpture in Former Yugoslavia Between Invisibility and Popularity. *II Lisbon Summer School of Culture / Peripheral Modernities.*

Jacobs, J. (2017) The Memorial at Srebrenica: Gender and the Social Meanings of Collective Memory in Bosnia-Herzegovina. *Memory Studies*, 10(4): 423–439.

Jameson, F. (1992) *Postmodernism, or, The Cultural Logic of Late Capitalism.* Durham: Duke University Press.

Jansen, S. (2015) *Yearnings in the Meantime: 'Normal Lives' and the State in a Sarajevo Apartment Complex.* New York: Berghahn.

Janson, H.W. (1976) *The Rise and Fall of the Public Monument.* New Orleans: The Graduate School, Tulane University.

Klein, N. (2007) *The Shock Doctrine.* New York: Metropolitan Books.

Kulić, V. (2018) Orientalizing Socialism: Architecture, Media, and the Representations of Eastern Europe. *Architectural Histories*, 6(1): 1–7.

Lefebvre, H. (1991) *The Production of Space.* Cambridge: Blackwell.

Levi, P. (2009) Kapo iz Omarske. *Beton* No 68. Available at: http://www.elektrobeton. net/strafta/kapo-iz-omarske/ (accessed 22 October 2018).

Lupu, N. (2003) Memory Vanished, Absent, and Confined: The Countermemorial Project in 1980s and 1990s Germany. *History & Memory*, 15(2): 130–164.

Mihaljević, D. (2018) *Zbogom avangardo: na razvalinama jugoslavenske socialističke Modernizacije.* Beograd: Rosa Luxemburg Stiftung Southeast Europe.

Mills, R. (2012) Commemorating a Disputed Past: Football Club and Supporter's Group War Memorials in the Former Yugoslavia. *History*, 97(328): 540–577.

Mitchell, W.J.T. (1992) The Violence of Public Art: Do the Right Thing. In Mitchell, W.J.T. (ed) *Art and the Public Sphere.* Chicago: University of Chicago Press, pp. 29–48.

Mujanović, J. (2014) The Baja Class and the Politics of Participation. In Arsenijević, Damirn (ed) *Unbribable Bosnia and Herzegovina: The Fight for the Commons.* Baden-Baden: Nomos, pp. 135–144.

Petrović, T. (2012) *Yuropa: Jugoslovensko Nasledje I Politike Buducnosti u Postjugoslovenskim Drustvima.* Beograd: Fabrika Knjiga.

Riegl, A. (1982) The Modern Cult of Monuments: Its Character and Its Origin. *Oppositions*, 25.

Ristić, M. (2018) *Architecture, Urban Space and War: The Destruction and Reconstruction of Sarajevo.* London: Palgrave Macmillan.

Sheftel, A. (2011) Monument to the International Community, from the Grateful Citizens of Sarajevo: Dark Humour as Counter-Memory in Post-Conflict Bosnia-Herzegovina. *Memory Studies*, 5(2): 145–164.

Sokol, A. (2014) War Monuments: Instruments of Nation-building in Bosnia and Herzegovina. *Croatian Political Science Review*, 51(5): 105–126.

Stevens, Q., Franck, K.A. and Fazakerley, R. (2012) Counter-Monuments: The Anti-Monumental and the Dialogic. *The Journal of Architecture*, 17(6): 951–972.

Sturken, M. (1998) Monuments: Historical Overview. In Kelly, Michael (ed) *Encyclopedia of Aesthetics*. New York: Oxford University Press, Volume 3.

Tello, V. (2016) *Counter-Memorial Aesthetics: Refugee Histories and the Politics of Contemporary Art*. London: Bloomsbury.

Thakkar, S. (2009) Transnational Memory Culture and the Countermonument Today. In *Memory Politics: Education, Memorials and Mass Media, Eleventh Berlin Roundtable on Transnationality*. Available at: http://www.irmgard-coninxstiftung. de/fileadmin/user_upload/pdf/Memory_Politics/Workshop_1/Thakkar_Essay.pdf.

Tomberger, C. (2010) The Counter-Monument: Memory Shaped by Male Post-War Legacies. In Paver, C.E. and Niven, W.J. (eds) *Memorialization in Germany since 1945*. London: Palgrave Macmillan, pp. 224–232.

UDIK (2018) *Spomenici I Politike Sjećanja U BiH I Republci Hrvatskoj: Kontroverze*. Sarajevo: UDIK.

Woodward, S. (1995) *Socialist Unemployment: The Political Economy of Yugoslavia 1945–1990*. Princeton: Princeton University Press.

Young, J. (1992) The Counter-Monument: Memory against Itself in Germany Today. *Critical Inquiry*, 18(2): 267–296.

Young, J. (ed) (1994) *The Art of Memory: Holocaust Memorials in History*. New York: Prestel.

Young, J. (1999) Memory and Counter-Memory. *Harvard Design Magazine No 9: Constructions of Memory: On Monuments Old and New*. Available at: http://www .harvarddesignmagazine.org/issues/9/memory-and-counter-memory.

Young, J. (2000) *At Memory's Edge: After-Images of the Holocaust in Contemporary Art and Architecture*. New Haven and London: Yale University Press.

Young, J. (2010) Memory and the Monument after 9/11. In Crownshaw, R., Kilby, J. and Rowland, A. (eds) *The Future of Memory*. New York: Berghahn, pp. 76–92.

2   Privatisation of History

Writing over a decade ago about post-socialist visual culture, Boris Groys suggested that its relation to the past can be described as privatisation (Groys 2008: 168). According to Groys, artists and cultural producers working in the context of post-socialism are able to tap into a large reservoir of symbols and images left over from communist times in order to bring complex and unfinished historical ideas and processes into the public conversation. And they are able to do so with relatively little effort because these symbols are still so meaningful to so many people. In identifying this process as privatisation, Groys drew a parallel between the still-present traces of socialist heritage, changes in conception of collective identity and the economic privatisation that has been taking place in post-socialist societies.

It appears that the privatisation of collective symbols from communist times continues unabated 30 years after the fall of the Berlin Wall. While this process can be observed across the former Eastern Bloc, the relation of countries of former Yugoslavia to their past – and their monuments in particular – in many ways represent its focal point: from systemic destruction, historical revisionism and denial of the socialist historical experience represented by the monuments (which can be seen as an example of privatisation through destruction) to the fetishisation of Yugoslav socialist-modernist monuments across the region and internationally as evidenced by the scores of publications, documentaries and the 2018–2019 MOMA exhibition about monuments and architecture in Socialist Yugoslavia (Kulić 2018). Yugoslav monuments are being assimilated into post-socialist narratives as ruins (ideological waste), heritage (rebranded as national monuments) or otherworldly aesthetic objects (Herscher 2015).

Seen in this context, Bosnia and Herzegovina (BiH) monuments built after 1996 are, unsurprisingly, most frequently thought and written about in terms of their relation to the large body of Yugoslav socialist monuments (Moll 2013; Sokol 2014; Burghardt and Kirn 2014; Čusto 2017; Pavlaković 2013). Whether it is in terms of erasure of history through the destruction of Mostar Partisan Necropolis, the appropriation and revision of history at Kozara or the opportunistic change of politics from socialism to nationalism by the Tjentište and Kragujevac monuments artist Miodrag Živković, Socialist Yugoslav World War II monuments continue to cast a long shadow over the present. In this sense, we can characterise the relation of post-conflict monumental construction in BiH to the past as privatisation of the legacy of monuments from the socialist era.

But what exactly is being privatised? While there is ample evidence about the way in which Yugoslav World War II monuments have been appropriated, destroyed or neglected, there is almost just as much to suggest that post-1996 BiH monuments are not in principle that much different from those built during the socialist era. This includes their proximity to the ideological agenda of the ruling party, through memorialisation of only 'our' victims (from the ideological point of view) to the promotion of a homogeneous version of history. Seemingly, while the ideological and aesthetic content of the monuments has seemingly changed, the form of memorialisation has in many ways stayed the same.

One way of understanding this process would be to suggest that the post-conflict monuments in BiH synthesise the worst aspects of Yugoslav Socialism and post-socialist neoliberalism. On the one hand, they continue the problematic synergy of monuments to the official ideology in Yugoslav Socialism (supporting the political process of 'nation building') including the intentional avoidance of facing complex historical questions of causality and historical responsibility. While being aimed at a clearly identifiable homogenous enemy – fascists and their local collaborators – the socialist monuments reflected the official silence on the inter-ethnic and religious violence in Yugoslavia during World War II. On the other hand, post-war monuments in BiH reflect the neoliberal privatisation and deregulation through their disregard of legal and aesthetic principles: they represent a monumental free market in which the ability to commemorate is not based on ethical, moral or aesthetic considerations, but on access to resources and proximity to political power. As the state withdraws, monument construction becomes a private enterprise. It is in this sense that BiH monuments embody the narrative of BiH transition into neoliberalism: they perfectly mirror not only the dramatic division and fragmentation of BiH along ethnonational and confessional differences (the permanent state of 'national crisis' enabling systemic corruption), but also the way in which this division is perpetuated by the ruling political parties as a way to obfuscate class differences and exploitation.

This chapter articulates the privatisation of history in post-conflict BiH monuments by looking at continuities and discontinuities between the current state of monuments and practices during and after Yugoslav Socialism. I discuss three forms of built structures that are crucial to understanding the emergence of post-conflict monuments in BiH: socialist monuments from Yugoslavia commemorating World War II anti-fascist Partisan struggle; private 'para-literature' tombstones used by individuals to commemorate their life while denouncing ungrateful families; and illegal and uncontrolled turbo-architecture that emerged in the wake of Yugoslavia's dissolution. While the relation of Socialist Yugoslav monuments to the present is relatively well known, the phenomena of tombstones and turbo-architecture as forms of para-legal built structures have been overlooked as key precedents for understanding the recent monument construction. I argue that they provide a way to explain both the privatisation of historical experience as well as deregulation of built environments into a grey economy. These three historical precedents also provide a timeline for official and unofficial public construction in Yugoslavia: most of the World War II monuments were built in the 1960–1970s, para-literature tombstones appear in the 1970–1980s and turbo-architecture emerges in the 1990s. They mark important points of change in the understanding of public memorial culture, and the increased role of private ownership of histories and commemorations following the fall of socialism in Yugoslavia.

In this respect, current monumental practices in BiH mark an intensification of processes and problems that were already present (and structurally inherent) in Yugoslav Socialism. But they also demonstrate a key point of difference, especially in relation to socialism monuments: their relation to temporality. I argue that the shift from socialist to nationalist narrative in monuments is not simply the process of erasure, destruction or revision of the past. And furthermore, that the shift from collective memories represented by the monuments to their privatised versions is not simply the shift from the universal to the singular. Rather, I argue that if taken together, they reflect a shift in the relation towards historical experience: an estrangement and distancing of Socialism into historical difference (Buden 2012). After outlining how each of the three historical precedents provides a political, aesthetic and legal framework for understanding the post-war monuments in BiH, I will return to the question of distancing historical experience through privatisation.

Turbo-architecture

In addition to the high number of monuments built in BiH since 1996, one of the more striking aspects of this development is how many of the monuments have been constructed without legal permits or approvals. According to reports, around 90% of current monuments have been constructed illegally (UDIK 2017), which would place their figure upwards of 1800 structures. One possible explanation for this number could be that it is another reflection of the systemic corruption and institutional dysfunction in BiH, where lines between legality and illegality are frequently blurred. However, given the high political and emotional stakes invested in the monuments, given their constant presence in the media and given their high visibility and ubiquity in everyday spaces of BiH, our answer may need to be more nuanced.

I have previously described the construction of monuments in BiH as an example of monumental free market, and in this section, I will clarify this term through the phenomenon of illegal and undocumented 'turbo-architecture' in 1990s Serbia, as a precedent for understanding the current legal framework for monument construction in BiH. I argue that the approach established by turbo-architecture construction – building without permits, building against regulations, erecting monuments in seemingly complete disregard of architectural or sculptural traditions – can be identified in BiH monuments' construction practices. I argue that this approach is enabled by the current laws regulating the construction of monuments in the Federation and Republika Srpska, albeit in slightly different ways. They both reflect the urge to build monuments in the grey space enabled by the state, and to establish private ownership over the recent past.

Turbo-architecture is a term used to describe the uncontrolled and illegal construction of buildings in Serbia during the Slobodan Milošević regime 1989–2000 (Jovanović-Weiss 2006). Enabled by Milošević's regime turning a blind eye to corruption, as many as 150,000 buildings, houses and additions were built in Belgrade from the time Milošević came to power in 1989 until he lost power on 5 October 2000. For a small fee (and a large bribe), city land across Serbia, but in Belgrade in particular – including sidewalks and land planned for highways – was made available for commercial and private construction. Turbo-architecture included commercial buildings, such as hotels, banks, gas stations and shopping centres, as well as private residences. These quickly built constructions incorporated diverse and incompatible styles, resulting in a trashy appearance that resembled the postmodernist experiments with pastiche. This was a case of accidental postmodernism achieved not through artistic or architectural practice, but through illegal construction with no quality control. Turbo-architecture provided a counterpoint to the history of architectural postmodernism by manifesting an aesthetic resemblance achieved completely externally to the disciplinary confines of theory and practice. Many examples of turbo-architecture are still visible around Serbia as material reminders of an architectural-ideological nexus that is ongoing.[1]

Illegal residential and commercial construction on a massive scale has been one of the many problems facing post-war BiH. While the issue of illegal construction dates back to the former Yugoslavia (Bežovan and Dakić 1990; Kos 1993) – including the authorities turning a blind eye to corruption – the post-war period has seen the exacerbation of the problem to rampant proportions (Fischer 2007: 39). Even a short trip through the country reveals a multitude of houses, apartment buildings, villas, restaurants, bars, petrol stations, motels, stores and shopping malls showing degrees of illegal or semi-legal construction. While this is somewhat less evident in larger urban centres such as Sarajevo, Tuzla, Mostar and Banja Luka, it is very visible in smaller and less developed areas.

As I suggested in the previous chapter, one notable example of turbo-architecture in BiH is the Šešlije Motel. Its garish mix of high-modernist minimalism with Chinese temple ornamentation is arresting and, in many ways, representative of a profusion of flamboyant, extravagant and chaotic housing across BiH (Kapetanović 2015). This kind of construction continues the lawlessness of turbo-architecture: from having a design that is completely at odds and incoherent with its surroundings, to permanently unfinished buildings with unpredictable completion dates. It stands as evidence of the collapse in planned and organised housing, especially relating to the question about the way in which construction permits were obtained.[2] Importantly, this kind of construction is common to the entire population of BiH and completely independent of ethnic or religious divisions. It is reflective of the increased wealth and political influence of individuals who were able to circumvent regulations. As I mentioned in the previous chapter, most of these buildings originated in the first phase of post-conflict reconstruction in BiH (1997–2008), and their appearance testifies to the chaotic illegality of privatised reconstruction during that period. It operates as the middle point between the nationalist traditionalism of the monuments and the influx of global capital in the form of highways, high-end apartment blocks and shopping centres.[3]

It is precisely at this middle point of the shift into twenty-first-century global capital that the turbo-architecture in BiH provides the aesthetic and economic background for post-conflict monuments. They exist on the same continuum of semi-legal or illegal construction carried out as private investment or initiative. The approach to construction established by turbo-architecture – where the regulators look away as long as it suits their agenda – has also been continued in BiH post-war monuments. This practice can be called deregulation of monuments' construction through legal non-enforcement.

In order to demonstrate how deregulation of monuments operates in BiH, we can observe the most frequent obstacle faced by victim associations, humanitarians and families from all three sides: if they are the ethnic minority in the local council, they will not be permitted to erect a monument or memorial plaque (UDIK 2017). There are numerous examples of intentional obstruction of monuments by the authorities, including the lack of progress in the construction of the memorial centre in Žepa village near Rogatica, the monument to murdered children of Prijedor and the memorial to JNA

(Yugoslav National Army) soldiers in Sarajevo. In each case, the association requesting construction permits is being blocked and obstructed by the local authorities. Across BiH, the authority over monument construction has been delegated to local councils – whether in the absence of a federal law, or whether through a calculated move – which act as the gate keepers. While delegating issuing of construction permits to local level authorities is standard practice in many places, in BiH it needs to be framed in the larger legal context, which creates a grey zone that enables construction.

At the federal level of BiH, there is no existing law that regulates the construction of monuments or memorials to the 1990s war. There are two laws that relate to aspects of monument construction. The existing *Law Protecting Heritage* covers buildings of 'national' historical or cultural significance but does not reflect on or even mention constructions after 1996 (Law Protecting Heritage). The marking of mass and individual grave locations is federally regulated by the *Rulebook for Marking of Sites of Exhumation and Burial of Missing Persons* (2006) (Službeni glasnik BiH 83/06). This document determines the standard for the appearance of the memorial and the financing of the memorial, such as the inclusion of biographical information, time of disappearance and time of exhumation. For marking a mass grave, the rulebook states that a committee will select an appropriate proposal. It also states that inscriptions are not to offend the religious or ethnic identity of other groups in BiH. While the document states the legal principles, the procedural problem with the rulebook is that according to the *Law about Missing Persons* (2004) (Službeni glasnik BiH 50/04), memorials are to be financed from a fund for helping families of missing persons, which was never established. What this demonstrates is that while legal principles are established, they are not enforced, creating an environment in which the logic of the free market can take over.

In the absence of federal (or state) law, local councils and municipalities in the Federation are the institutions that issue permits for construction and approvals. Sarajevo is perhaps the exception here, because its construction of monuments is regulated and centralised. However, even in Sarajevo there are examples of nationalist usurping of monuments. As Ristić demonstrates, in a number of cases of monuments not conceived as reflective of nationalism, such as the *Memorial to Children Killed in the Siege of Sarajevo* 1992–1995, interest groups end up monopolising the projects and reframing them through the nationalist lens (Ristić 2018). This demonstrates the inability or unwillingness of the authorities to censor the nationalist rhetoric despite the (semblance of) existing legal framework. Similarly, while the Brčko District has a *Law About Monuments and Symbols of Brčko District* (2003), which includes clauses forbidding offensive or provocative symbols on monuments, as I will show, this did not prevent the erection of a monument to Draža Mihailović on the land owned by the Serbian Orthodox Church.

Republika Srpska has a law from 2011 regulating monuments and memorials to 'liberation wars' on the territories of RS (*Law About Monuments and Memorials to Liberation Wars*). On the one hand, the law very clearly defines the ethnonational parameters of what is acceptable, including 'meaningful events from liberation wars', 'nurturing of cultural-historical tradition' and 'honouring fallen Serb and Montenegrin soldiers in liberation wars until 1918, WWII antifascist struggle, and homeland war for Republika Srpska'.[4] On the other hand, the law stipulates that the approval of monument construction is made at the 'local' level, giving the legal jurisdiction to the local unit in cooperation with veterans' associations.[5] Furthermore, while Clauses 25–27 of the Law clearly stipulate the requirement to establish and maintain a central register of monuments, this has not yet eventuated. This means that 'local' (city) authorities determine the list which are of cultural significance in cohort with veteran associations, which are overwhelmingly Serb nationalists. In other words, while monument construction in Republika Srpska is seemingly regulated, the decision-making process is framed in such a way that it is always politicised and uncritical towards the Serb narrative.[6] A good example of the politics behind monument construction in Republika Srpska is the Prijedor municipality where over 3100 Bosniak people died during the war, including over 100 murdered children. Despite numerous initiatives by activists and academics to build monuments to victims, the local government is not even considering their proposals (N1 2018).

Given this legal framework, the monumental free market in BiH operates as a 'grey space' between legality and illegality (Yiftachel 2009). In the context of BiH monuments, this grey space defines the ambiguity between the legal framework for monuments as set out by law, the process of giving permits for construction and the actual construction of monuments. While at face value there is nothing suspicious about the local authorities deciding about local monuments, the evidence of systemic discrimination against monuments dedicated to non-majority ethnic groups suggests otherwise. It appears that the presence of political actors – such as veterans associations' representatives, members of political parties or members of the clergy – on all council boards is a way to ensure that only certain kinds of monuments are accepted.[7] Furthermore, while the legal framework, where it exists, defines the cultural significance of monuments, the evidence on the ground demonstrates that the approval of monuments involves no quality control or presence of cultural experts on any of the panels. BiH monuments thus fall into the grey space of illegal development that is enabled through the withdrawal of the state. Crucially, this withdrawal does not mean a greater deal of autonomy from the official ideology. Rather, grey space becomes an increased locus of power, which usually appears in specific moments, usually in tune with election cycles.

This grey space of the state enabling and disabling monument projects on an ideological and political basis is illustrated by two examples. In 2012, the Islamic Association in Višegrad erected a monument to Bosniaks, which used the word 'genocide' in its inscription. Despite being located on private property of the Islamic Association, the Serb authorities forcibly removed the word from the inscription in 2014. By comparison, after the introduction of the 2003 law regulating the construction of monuments in the Brčko District, which prevents discrimination on the basis of religious or ethnic identity, the monument to Četnik General Draža Mihailović was removed from the centre of town. The statue of the Mihailović was made in Belgrade in 1991, and inaugurated in Vukovar in 1992. When Vukovar passed from 'Serb' to 'Croat' hands, the monument was returned to Belgrade, and in 1998 it was installed in Brčko. In 2003, the Brčko District enacted a Law on Monuments and Symbols which stipulated that only those monuments 'based on the equality of all constitutive peoples' may be erected in public places, and the monument was removed. In 2004, a new monument to the Četnik leader appeared in the Brčko Orthodox cemetery, which is owned by the Serbian Orthodox Church. The monument was erected by the Ravna Gora Četnik Movement of Republika Srpska, and the Church contributed the land. These examples illustrate the way in which the legal framework for monuments in BiH slips between respecting and disregarding private property based on ideological priorities.[8]

Para-literature Tombstones

If turbo-architecture helps to explain the way in which post-war monuments operate in the grey space of existing laws and regulations concerning monuments in BiH, para-literature tombstones help us to explain the lack of sensitivity and empathy to 'the other side'. One of the frequently heard criticisms of the monuments is the way in which they establish a binary between 'our' victims and the homogenised (often unseen) 'other side'. Terms such as 'aggressors' 'and 'criminals' are frequently used in inscriptions on monuments to describe who the fallen were fighting and amplify their martyrdom through nationalist rhetoric of independence. Further, the location of many monuments is intentionally chosen to be in proximity of contentious sites of violence, even if that monument is not directly addressing the event. In an immediate sense, they illustrate the ongoing presence of nationalism in how the war is remembered, and how national interests are used to frame the post-war reality in BiH.

Yet, this emphasis on nationalism possibly overlooks the fact that the form of memorialisation on post-war monuments also continues older traditions. Nationalist 'othering' is fused with existing forms of memorialisation, and normalised as their logical extension. Here I want to propose a reading of the monuments that will move beyond the nationalist framework, and reframe the nationalism expressed by the monuments as an intersection of mourning and a private version of history. Because so many of the newly constructed monuments negotiate between public and private memories, because so many are built outside of the state regulations, they mediate between traditions of private mourning, and public proclamations of nationalism.

On the one hand, this will help to account for the large number of smaller memorials and memorial plaques, which aesthetically often resemble gravestones, and are often found in cemeteries. But on the other hand, this will also help to explain the forms of memorialisation evident in larger and more visible structures, which often resembles cemetery memorials. Put differently, my argument is that all structures have the same form of memorialisation, which draws on forms of mourning found in 'para-literature tombstones' more than they draw on modernist monuments from Socialist Yugoslavia. Crucially, it is not my intention to deny the blatant and offensive nationalism of many of these monuments, but to position it within a longer history of commemoration that operated on the margins of legality.

What are 'para-literature tombstones'? They are a form of self-memorialisation identified in Serbian anthropologist Ivan Čolović's study of new epitaphs on gravesites around Serbia in the early 1980s, which in addition to the basic biographical information about the deceased and mourners (name, dates) contained a form of narration and commentary about the life and death of the deceased (Čolović 1985: 7). This commentary took the form of quotes, poems or song lyrics intended to capture the deceased's life and narrate the events leading to their death.

Čolović suggests that the epitaphs used forms of social address in line with established peasant traditions and village customs that could be traced back to the late nineteenth and early twentieth century Serbia: public communication of grief to establish belonging to social and familial groups (Čolović 1985: 11). In this form of communication, the deceased takes the position of an active participant and speaker in dialogue with the living by narrating the circumstances of their death or by thanking the living for their visit. These epitaphs functioned as a form of chronologies or news updates that relayed documentary and anecdotal events. Čolović argues that the epitaphs built on the traditions by using (then) contemporary popular music lyrics and lines from poems to communicate the magnitude of the suffered loss or the process of mourning.

Čolović describes the epitaphs as examples of para-literature (divlja književnost) (Čolović 1985: 63): applied literature subjugated to a specific purpose. The use of song lyrics or poetry on epitaphs transforms the poetry and lyrics from their original meaning into messages exchanged between the dead and the living, the mourners and the public. Čolović argues that this use of literature has two important consequences for our understanding of literature as a genre. First, the repurposing of poetry of lyrics into new and unexpected contexts removes them from their original meaning, thereby limiting their use as a 'genre' of literature. Second, this process also frees them from the constraints of literature as a discourse and institution and returns them to what Čolović describes as an artistically irrelevant but socio-psychologically vital destructive-constructive process of symbolic folkloric communication (Čolović 1985: 63).

Čolović's account needs to be understood in the context of broader historical discussions about the relation of artistic production and everyday life. While some of his claims reflect their historical and theoretical contexts – poststructuralist understanding of the symbolic structure of literature, and Pierre Bourdieu's account of class expressed through taste – his account was nevertheless the first attempt to theoretically articulate vernacular cultural artefacts that emerged in the 1980s Yugoslavia. Čolović articulates gravestone epitaphs, newspaper personals and newly composed folk music (NCFM) as reflective of marginal identities experimenting with traditional cultural forms in the context of rapid modernisation.[9] On the one hand, Čolović argues that the stylistic experimentation, transformation and departure from the 'ideal' of folklore in these forms of cultural communication was often perceived from the top as a form of cultural degeneration (Čolović 1985: 149). On the other hand, he argues that the majority of producers came from lower socio-economic backgrounds with limited access to education. Čolović shows that the perceived aesthetic inferiority of these cultural artefacts and modes of expression (tombstones and NCFM in particular) is expressive of a sociocultural differentiation between the working class and the cultural intelligentsia in Yugoslavia (Čolović 1985: 147).

Seen in this context, para-literature tombstones can be understood as artefacts that mediated the cultural and personal memory of the displaced workers who moved from rural to urban centres of Yugoslavia seeking employment. In other words, they are the cultural expression of the marginalised working class in the economic, social and cultural liberalisation of Yugoslavia in the 1960 and 1970s: the origin of Yugoslavia's post-socialist transition into neo-liberalism (Dimitrijević 2016).

Since Čolović's study, para-literature tombstones started appearing at an even higher rate in cemeteries in Serbia and BiH. Artist Mladen Miljanović used tombstone engravings as source material for his work *The Garden of Earthly Delights* (2013), which represented BiH at the 2013 Venice Biennale through posthumous pleasures, desires and hopes of everyday people (Čvoro 2018). In his research for the project, Miljanović identified the 1980s as the period when hyper-realistic portraits of the deceased start appearing on tombstones of all ethnic groups and in cemeteries across BiH. Enlarged photographs of the deceased were transferred onto the stone and engraved as a way to reflect their life and personality through the punctum of that image. The production of these tombstones further increased in the 1990s, where they also started to include the favourite activity of the deceased, their precious possessions (cars, musical instruments, hunting gear), objects that represent their profession (e.g. shepherd, policeman, chef, pilot) or passion in life (e.g. dancing, singing, horse-riding). These engravings offered a non-solemn, colloquial approach to commemorating death through attempts at symbolic immortality (Curseu and Pop-Curseu 2011: 374). In some cases, they include representations of activities that went beyond the presumed sanctity of death: I have seen a tombstone engraving of an elderly couple preparing a dead pig for a spit roast; an image of an obese man eating a whole chicken; and a couple whose tombstone is accompanied by 3D printouts of their heads.

More importantly to our present discussion, from the 1980s certain tombstones also included engraved declarations by the deceased rejecting their ungrateful families over money or property squabbles. One particular tombstone in Serbia features a long statement listing the grievances committed on her by her family and proclaiming that she is 'erecting this monument to herself'. In the form of a last statement, the deceased frames her life as a struggle of hard work in Germany that was never appreciated by her greedy family. This example illustrates the practice of public denunciation of family as the final message, colloquially known as 'inat' (spite) monuments.

The use of the word 'inat' is significant in that it signals a range of historical, cultural and psychological factors. Originally a Turkish word meaning 'persistence', it has become a colloquial loan word used to describe 'intentional, provocative, defiant behaviour towards someone or something' (Nikolić 2007: 471). Although clearly a universal human trait, best described in English as 'defiance for the sake of defiance rather than to achieve a long-term goal', in the region of the former Yugoslavia 'inat' is usually associated with Serbs and qualified as 'Serbian inat' (Glenny). This has led to the idea that Serbs have internalised 'inat' as a 'national characteristic' in their recent history, which presumably explained the aggressive assertion of Serb dominance over BiH, Croatia and Kosovo throughout the 1990s, and the stubborn defiance of the NATO bombing campaign of Serbia in 1999. However, it has also been suggested that the language and cultural perception of 'inat' in Serbia was used and manipulated by Slobodan Milošević to create populist hysteria and maintain political control.

The term 'inat monuments' has been used to describe several post-war monuments in BiH, which use language or symbolism intended to provoke or offend members of other ethnic groups, or whose location can be interpreted as a provocation. Perhaps the archetypal inat monument in BiH is the monument to Serb fighters in Petkovci Village, built in the shape of the Serb nationalist three-finger salute near a location of mass murder of Bosniaks.[10]

The cultural essentialism of framing 'inat' as predominantly Serb is important to bear in mind when thinking about monuments. Even though there is a disproportionally larger number of 'inat monuments' created by the Serbs in BiH, it is by no means exclusive to Serbs.[11] Further, as Čolović demonstrates, the traditions of commemorating the dead through writing and illustrating of tombstones are most pronounced with the Serbs, meaning that they would be most likely to use tombstone monuments to send messages of defiance. More importantly, we need to distinguish between 'inat tombstones' as individual acts of defiance by the deceased usually directed at their family, and 'inat monuments', which are representations of groups of deceased and directed at national 'others'.

In discussing the individual psychology of inat, Serbian ethnologist Bojan Jovanović argues that to do something out of inat means to oppose for the sake of opposition and to manifest our will rather than achieve an outcome (Jovanović 2008: 116). Inat is a form of conscious irrational and juvenile rebellion towards the environment, which symbolically punishes others through a self-destructive act. In this sense, erecting a tombstone to oneself which intentionally makes a mockery out of death by listing our grievances with those closest to us is intended to punish the family by defiling commemoration. The author of the tombstone is aware that their gesture will have no effect other than to make a mockery out of their life and family 'in eternity'. Their conscious decision to defy the 'sanctity' of commemoration is a way to defy death through a negation of life.

In considering inat tombstones as precedents for post-conflict monuments, it is important to ask how many 'inat' tombstones have been dictated by the will of the deceased, and how many are changed by the family after they passed away. This question becomes even more pronounced where inat tombstones are erected 'for' the deceased, without any sense of what the deceased would have thought about such instrumentalisation of their death. Chapter 3 will look at specific examples to discuss the consequences of mixing personal grief and grievance of 'inat' tombstones with toxic nationalist politics. Here we can suggest that a key aspect of post-war inat monuments is their expression of neoliberal temporality, including accelerationism (the speeding up of production and higher volume of monuments) and fragmentation (subjecting public commemorative practices according to private interests, which are rejecting tradition and family bonds). Importantly, the hyper-individualised subjectivity that is emerging through inat monuments is manifesting and expressing itself through the framework of the nation, thus joining nineteenth-century nationalism with twenty-first-century neoliberalism.

Socialist Monuments and Modernism

As I noted earlier, the post-war monuments in BiH – as indeed all monuments built across the former Yugoslavia since its dissolution – stand in the shadows of socialist monuments of Yugoslavia. Built in the 1960s and 1970s through a state initiative, socialist monuments in Yugoslavia occupied a significant portion of the public sphere in urban and rural areas and stood as key symbols of collective identification that drew upon collective socialist experiences (Horvatinčić 2018). Despite attempts to erase them from memory or physically destroy them, they remain as key factors in popular consciousness.

In an immediate sense, their presence remains because of their striking and highly idiosyncratic appearance, which fuses large-scale monumentalism with high modernist abstraction and site-specificity. On the level of appearance, monuments built after 1996 pale in comparison to the grandiose symbolism of Socialist Yugoslav monuments.

Yet, in terms of their relationship to the ruling ideology, the BiH monuments are in principle not that much different to the socialist monuments. The war monuments built in Socialist Yugoslavia also reflected a grand historical narrative, promoting only one version of history and memorialising only 'our' victims ('our' from the ideological point of view). They suited the ideological agenda of the ruling Communist Party, which sanctioned monumentalisation and interpretation of the past and history.[12] From a historical distance, it is easy to forget that these monuments often constituted an uncritical affirmation, mythologisation and hyper-production of places of memory that commemorated the constitutive moments of the political regime: People's Liberation Struggle, the socialist revolution, and the tradition of social uprising and the workers' movement. Yet, even though the Yugoslav model of constructing social memory was overtly ideologically defined, marked by examples of selective memory and politically motivated gradation of importance when it came to specific historical episodes, essentially it was not much different from the politics of memory in other European countries.

Further, there is a great deal of similarity between how commemorating the past is mediated through BiH monuments and Yugoslav socialist monuments. They both constitute a form of war-centric memory, where military cartography plays a central role in constructing and transferring of memory. Territory as one of the central places of war memory in Yugoslavia was understood as an authentic spatial unit marked by the experience of war (battles, execution sites, concentration camps, secret military bases) that had to be preserved and permanently marked by using various strategies of design, which would help transfer the memory of war to the future generations. Ownership of space continues to play a central part in the positioning of post-war monuments in BiH, both through marking sites of violence and by marking territorial gains.

But this also relates to the different kinds of memories that are mediated by the monuments. We can observe this by drawing on Heike Karge's account of official and unofficial commemorative practices in post-World War II Yugoslavia (Karge 2009). Karge argues that much like Yugoslavia, which stood politically wedged between the Eastern Bloc and Western Bloc, socialist monuments attempted to mediate a series of symbolic and aesthetic gaps. Karge suggests the term 'mediation of remembrance' to articulate 'the field in which personal grief, local practices, cultural codes and political desiderata to commemorate the past will merge' (Karge 2009: 50). From Karge's account can be extrapolated three different, yet interconnected, levels of mediation. These three points of mediation are located between official and local identity, between the historicism of socialism and its future orientation and between remembering and historical amnesia.

Following World War II, Yugoslav identity was positioned between pan-Yugoslav shared identity and regional ethnic identity, and socialist monuments presented mediation points between commemoration practices sanctioned by the state and localised practices of remembering. While the state commissioned and financed most of the large and well-known monuments across Yugoslavia, which were large minimalist steel and concrete abstract works, two-thirds of all memorials were erected in the name of local remembrance and featured figurative sculptures of local war heroes. The gap between the official and local practices of commemoration became the staple of the monuments' symbolic economy. Socialist monuments did not merely represent the merging of official and local practices, but rather were commemorations regulated by regional political interests and representation. The local hero was not the sign of the collective, but a site of connections and disjunctions within the official narrative.

Second, socialist monuments were sites that articulated the experience of history, not in terms of linear narratives, but as the compounding of past, present and future. While socialist monuments symbolised the sacrifices of the past in the struggle against fascism and oppression, they simultaneously symbolised the end of history through socialist revolution, and the seeds for a socialist future. The retro-futuristic style of many of the monuments served as a reminder of past struggles and the enormous collective loss and pain inflicted by the war, and yet also served to articulate a future-oriented narrative that expressed how these struggles achieved liberation, progress and socialist revolution.

The third (and the most contentious) level of mediation in socialist monuments centred on how these monuments celebrate the victory over fascism, while not naming local collaborators or former enemies. The monuments were abstract in order to be representative of a complex history without directly acknowledging historical responsibility, thereby figuring abstraction as a reflection of the difficulty of commemorating a war of liberation. The difficulty in representing historical responsibility came because the civil conflict was fought along tangled political and ethnic lines, after which both victims and perpetrators had to unite to collectively form the Socialist Republic of Yugoslavia.

These three levels of mediation in socialist monuments are repeated in the post-war BiH monuments. Almost all the monuments were built through local initiatives and intended to be symbolic of the plight of local communities in the absence of, and incredulity towards, official historical narratives. As such, they represent mediation points between the state's refusal to deal with the recent past and localised practices of remembering. In this sense, the importance of the local site becomes even more pronounced in post-conflict monuments. Monuments are dedicated to local people who gave their lives to defending specific cities or neighbourhoods. This includes monuments to people which often have connections to the criminal underworld, or have been accused of war crimes. But this is romanticised within the narrative of the local as protection representing authenticity and tradition.

Therefore, we can identify that there are significant continuities between the two periods, returning us to the question of what is the difference between them? I argue that this difference can be found in their relation to temporality.

As Kirn (2012) argues, the difference between post-Yugoslav memory and the Yugoslav socialist modernist memory relates both to the subjectivity addressed in their respective memorials and to their temporality. Socialist modernist memorials in particular strove towards a future and the possibility of a different world; rather than asserting the fixed past, they remain open to history as a set of contingent processes. Moreover, they went beyond a subjectivity that is based on exclusionary categories. In post-socialist times, memorials address local fascists, the nation, Christianity – all denominators of the presupposed subjectivity. Subjectivity in the partisan memorials was centred instead around the abstract figuration of the community to come, working people and partisans who would re-activate the history of the oppressed. Post-war BiH memory focuses on the romantic teleological temporality of the nation with its strong ethnic and religious form of identification. In its most extreme variant, nationalist reconciliation takes the form of a defence of fascism and local collaboration.

***

In outlining the continuities and discontinuities between the present and previous ideological systems in BiH, my intention in this chapter was to show the nationalist-neoliberal nexus underpinning the privatisation of history in monuments. Privatisation of history is the narrative of historical correction that emerges in the wake of the end of socialism. Identities that emerge after the end of socialism are presented as repressed during the totalitarian reign. Nationalism emerges as the primary mode of identification, which is conflated with the notion of individual freedom and private ownership. This right is expressed through para-literature tombstones' attempt to control the narrative of their life against the conventions of commemoration. This right is also expressed in the grey space enabled by the legal framework, which makes it possible for anyone with the means to build a monument, regardless of ethical or moral implications of the act. Privatisation of history in BiH monuments thus distances and defamiliarises Socialism into a historical difference (Buden 2012). Socialism becomes a historical experience but not 'our' historical experience; the past is recognised only as difference.

Notes

1   Turbo-architecture did not cease after the fall of Milošević. Despite being outright rejected by both sides of the political spectrum in Serbia, turbo-architecture was paradoxically promoted as a new national style at the Venice Architecture Biennale in 2002, as proof of endurance against the 1999 NATO bombing of Serbia.
2   The owner of the motel is a high-ranking police officer from Doboj, which raises the question of how the council permit was obtained. While there is no evidence that the motel is a continuation of systemic corruption that produced turbo-architecture, it is impossible to imagine such a building passing through a professional council panel assessment.
3   The most recent example is the *Delta* Shopping Centre, which was opened in Banja Luka in March 2019, and is the largest shopping centre in BiH.
4   The original clause is:

> Zaštita, održavanje i izgradnja spomenika i spomen-obilježja iz čl. 1. i 2. ovog zakona provodi se u cilju trajnog obilježavanja značajnih događaja oslobodilačkih ratova, čuvanja uspomena na istaknute ličnosti oslobodilačkih ratova, njegovanja kulturno-istorijske tradicije i odavanja počasti poginulim pripadnicima Srpske i Crnogorske vojske u oslobodilačkim ratovima do 1918. godine, učesnicima antifašističke borbe u Drugom svjetskom ratu, kao i borcima u Odbrambeno-otadžbinskom ratu Republike Srpske.

(Član 3)

5   The original clause is:

> Listu spomenika i spomen-obilježja od velikog značaja za jedinicu lokalne samouprave utvrđuje opštinski/gradski organ uprave nadležan za poslove boračko-invalidske zaštite u saradnji sa Boračkom organizacijom Republike Srpske, Republičkom organizacijom porodica zarobljenih i poginulih boraca i nestalih civila Republike Srpske i Savezom udruženja boraca NOR-a Republike Srpske.

(Član 10)

6 This is evident in the list of objects of cultural-historical significance www.naslje dje.org/sr_RS/kutlrunoistorisjko

7 This includes the construction of monuments that are dedicated to foreign mercenaries which took part in the war. Two examples that illustrate this point are the monument to mujahedeen in Livade village near Zavidovići, and the monument to Russian volunteers near Višegrad.

8 It should be noted that the grey space of the law regulating monuments has also been used by activist groups to subvert the nationalist narrative of monuments. Activist group 'Jer Me Se Tiče' (Becasue it Concerns Me), led by Emir Hodžić, erected overnight makeshift monuments in Prijedor in protest of Serb authorities' refusal to allow commemorations of genocide against Bosniaks. After the monuments were removed by the local police, Hodžić and the group demanded their return because they were private property.

9 I discuss newly composed folk music in Čvoro 2014.

10 I will examine this monument in more detail in Chapter 3.

11 Another example of inat monuments can be found in the destruction of the monument to ARBiH fighters in front of the Mostar city council. As ARBiH is seen by the Croats in Mostar as a predominantly Bosniak military formation, the monument was seen as a provocation, destroyed by explosives and replaced by a monument to the Croat HVO.

12 As Igor Zabel argues, from the 1950s onward, there was a symbiosis between modernist art and the party-state apparatus, in which modernist art was supported and used to promote the public image of the state (Zabel 2018). This is especially evident in the large number of monuments to the revolution that were directly commissioned by the state. In 1980, Yugoslavia appeared at the Venice Biennale with the theme of monuments (which Zabel actually calls 'modernist landscape sculptures') and presented a picture of a country in which the socialist system was combined with a high level of modernist art. This event is a parallel to the showing of turbo-architecture by Serbia at the architectural Venice Biennale. State using modernism and state using postmodernism.

References

Bežovan, G. and Dakić, S. (1990) *Alternativna stambena politika*. Zagreb: Radničke novine.

Buden, B. (2012) *Zona Prelaska: O Kraju Postkomunizma*. Beograd: Fabrika Knjiga.

Burghardt, R. and Kirn, G. (2014) Hybrid Memorial Architecture and Objects of Revolutionary Aesthetics. In Dunn, A. and MacPhee, J. (eds) *Signal 03*. Oakland: PM Press, pp. 99–131.

Čolović, I. (1985) *Divlja Knjizevnost*. Beograd: Nolit.

Curseu, Petru Lucian and Pop-Curseu, Ioan (2011) Alive after Death: An Exploratory Cultural Artifact Analysis of the Merry Cemetery of Sapanta. *Journal of Community & Applied Social Psychology*, 21: 371–387.

Čusto, A. (2017) Spomenici i prakse sjećanja u Bosni i Hercegovini. *Zbornik Radova Historijskog Muzeja Bosne I Hercegovine*. 12: 60–69.

Čvoro, U. (2014) *Turbo-folk Music and Cultural Representations of National Identity in Former Yugoslavia*. London: Ashgate.

Čvoro, U. (2018) *Transitional Aesthetics: Contemporary Art at the Edge of Europe.* London: Bloomsbury.

Dimitrijević, B. (2016) *Potrošeni Socijalizam: Kultura, Konzumerizam i Društvena Imaginacija u Jugoslaviji (1950–1974).* Beograd: Fabrika Knjiga.

Fischer, M. (2007) Moving out of the Dayton Era into the Era of Brussels? In Fischer, Martina (ed) *Peacebuilding and Civil Society in Bosnia-Herzegovina: Ten Years after Dayton.* Berlin: Lit Verlag.

Glenny, M. Untranslatable: Inat. Available at: http://wwword.com/2685/words/untranslatable/inat/ (accessed 22 October 2018).

Groys, B. (2008) *Art Power.* Cambridge: MIT.

Herscher, A. (2015) From the Politics of Memory to the Memory of Politics: The Socialist Monument in and after Yugoslavia. Paper presented at conference *Memorial For(u)ms–Histories of Possibility,* 3–4 July 2015, Berlin.

Horvatinčić, S. (2018) Memorial Sculpture and Architecture in Socialist Yugoslavia. In Kulić, V. and Stierli, M. (eds) *Toward a Concrete Utopia: Architecture in Yugoslavia, 1948–1980.* New York: The Museum of Modern Art, pp. 104–111.

Jovanović, B. (2008) *Prkos I Inat: Etnopsihološke studije.* Beograd: Zavod za udžbenike.

Jovanović-Weiss, S. (2006) *Almost Architecture.* Stuttgart: Merz & Solitude.

Kapetanović, M. (2015) Post-Socialist Landscape: A Castle by the Road. *Studia Ethnologica Croatica,* 27: 449–478.

Karge, H. (2009) Mediated Remembrance: Local Practices of Remembering the Second World War in Tito's Yugoslavia. *European Review of History,* 16(1): 49–62.

Kirn, G. (2012) Transformation of Memorial Sites in the Post-Yugoslav Context. In Šuber, Daniel and Karamanić, Slobodan (eds) *Retracing Images: Visual Culture after Yugoslavia.* Leiden and Boston: Brill, pp. 251–281.

Kos, D. (1993) Predmodernost ali postmodernost "črnograditeljskih" praks. *Teorija in praksa* 5/6: 453–458.

Kulić, V. (2018) Orientalizing Socialism: Architecture, Media, and the Representations of Eastern Europe. *Architectural Histories,* 6(1): 1–7.

Law About Missing Persons (2004) Available at: http://ckks.ba/pdf/Zakon%20o%20nestalim%20osobama%20BiH%20-%202004.pdf (accessed 16 October 2018).

Law About Monuments and Memorials to Liberation Wars. Available at: http://www.narodnaskupstinars.net/?q=la/akti/usvojeni-zakoni/zakon-o-spomenicima-i-spomen-obilježjima-oslobodilačkih-ratova (accessed 16 October 2018).

Law About Monuments and Symbols of Brčko District (2003) Available at: https://skupstinabd.ba/3-zakon/ba/Zakon%20o%20spomenicima%20i%20simbolima%20Brc--ko%20Distrikta%20BiH/000%2022-03%20Zakon%20o%20spomenicima%20i%20simbolima%20Brc--ko%20Ditrikta.pdf (accessed 16 October 2018).

Law Protecting Heritage Deemed by the Commission for the Protection of National Monuments as National Monuments. Available at: https://www.fmks.gov.ba/kultura/legislativa/fbih/71.pdf (accessed 16 October 2018).

Moll, N. (2013) Fragmented Memories in a Fragmented Country: Memory Competition and Political Identity-Building in Today's Bosnia and Herzegovina. *Nationalities Papers,* 41(6): 910–935.

N1 (2018) Available at: http://ba.n1info.com/a280011/Vijesti/Vijesti/Inzkov-odg ovor-o-spomeniku-u-Prijedoru.html (accessed 18 October 2018).

Nikolić, M. (ed) (2007) *Rečnik Srpskog Jezika*. Novi Sad: Matica Srpska.

Pavlaković, V. (2013) Symbols and the Culture of Memory in Republika Srpska Krajina. *Nationalities Papers: The Journal of Nationalism and Ethnicity*, 41(6): 893–909.

Ristić, M. (2018) *Architecture, Urban Space and War: The Destruction and Reconstruction of Sarajevo*. London: Palgrave Macmillan.

Službeni glasnik BiH broj 50/04 (2004) Zakon o nestalim osobama. Available at: http://www.sluzbenilist.ba/page/i/7VG6VEINp4Y= (accessed 18 October 2018).

Službeni glasnik BiH broj 83/06 (2006) Pravilnik o Obilježavanju mjesta iskopavanja I ukopa nestalih osoba. Available at: http://www.sluzbenilist.ba/page/i/gztz5k 76kjn45hbF1ViICohz4nh78h773A= (accessed 18 October 2018).

Sokol, A. (2014) War Monuments: Instruments of Nation-building in Bosnia and Herzegovina. *Croatian Political Science Review*, 51(5): 105–126.

UDIK (2017) *The Association for Social Research and Communications Central Register of Monuments*. Sarajevo: UDIK.

Yiftachel, O. (2009) Critical Theory and 'Gray Space': Mobilization of the Colonized. *City*, 13(2–3): 240–256.

Zabel, I. (2018) Art and State: From Modernism to the Retro-Avant Garde. In Janevski, Ana, Marocci, Roxana and Nouril, Ksenia (eds) *Art and Theory of Post-1989 Central and Eastern Europe: A Critical Anthology*. Durham: Duke, pp. 49–52.

3 Temporal Formations of BiH Post-Conflict Monuments

In the hyper-production of monuments in Bosnia and Herzegovina (BiH), an overwhelming emphasis is on producing three separate and distinctive national histories and identities, and projecting ownership over territory. Thousands of monuments built since 1996 dot the landscape of a relatively small country, dispersed across town and village streets and squares, cemeteries and places of religious worship, and remote sites of atrocities. These monuments were built through initiatives from veteran associations, families of victims, citizens associations, nongovernmental organisations (NGOs), religious and local communities and local authorities, and funded through municipal or ministerial budgets or through private donations.[1] In many cases, these monuments are constructed without public competition, public debate or participation by artists. This is reflected in traditionalist aesthetics of the large majority of the structures with easily recognisable didactic religious and national identity symbols such as flags, emblems or other national insignia.[2]

This process indicates an instrumentalised use of monuments in the service of glorifying militaristic, masculine and exclusive national pasts, which has been well-documented and discussed in the existing literature. In an immediate sense, the ideological 'curators' of national identities in contemporary BiH use monuments to shape not only the vexed history of the 1992–1995 conflict, but also reach for deeper histories such as the still- unresolved history of anti-fascist struggle in World War II, Socialist Yugoslavia as material to be revised in the service of national history. Heated discussions about the war in the 1990s, genocide, anti-fascism and fascism, communism and nationalism are an almost daily occurrence in BiH public life, often triggered by the appearance of yet another monument, the renaming of another school or street after an indicted war criminal or commemoration of another controversial historical figure.[3]

In this context, it would appear very difficult to imagine that there is any other way to interpret this complex tangle other than as an expression of nationalism. In fact, it is often the case that even forms of commemoration that attempt to move beyond the national framework get sequestered into nationalist discourses. Mirjana Ristić's account of post-war commemoration in Sarajevo demonstrates the way in which public reactions to monuments that were intended as gestures against nationalism created divisions (Ristić 2018). The public debate over the *Memorial to Children Killed in the Siege of Sarajevo* 1992–1995 (*Spomen-obilježje ubijenoj djeci opkolje-nog Sarajeva 1992–1995*) (2009) located in a public park in central Sarajevo turned towards whether it should commemorate 'our' or 'their' children. Also, Sarajevo Roses – traces of mortar explosions on streets and pavements filled with red wax – were intended as silent reminders of all victims of the Sarajevo siege (Kurto 2006). Despite all absence of 'official' support, markings or any didactic explanations, they continue to be perceived as provocations by members of the public (Kappler 2017).[4]

In Chapter 1, I outlined the way in which the monumentalisation of BiH legitimises the transition to neoliberalism in the guise of nationalism. I argued that the overwhelming focus on nationalism as the interpretative framework for understanding the construction of monuments and their visual language overlooks how neoliberalism has become the unquestioned framework and the enabling force for nationalism. In Chapter 2, I also argued that rather than a complete break with the past, the current process of monumentalisation in many ways marks a continuation of earlier forms, albeit with historical temporality as a significant difference. I argued that the monuments constructed after 1996 position the past as difference, which is estranged and distanced from the present.

Building on the argument that post-war monuments in BiH provide a reconfiguration of time in line with neoliberalism, and extending my claim that they constitute three variations on the same culture of remembrance, this chapter will outline four temporal formations through which monuments can be understood. This chapter articulates how the temporal formations of leap, loss, return and delay in BiH monuments relate to the teleology from 'authentic' national history to neoliberal free market.[5] Leap is reflected in monuments that circumvent the 40 years of socialism and the legacy of anti-fascism in BiH (as empty time) and connect the present to the national past in a straight line: manipulation of Narodno Oslobodilačka Borba or NOB (People's Liberation Struggle) and BiH as an anti-fascist political project. Loss is reflected in 'inat' monuments that instrumentalise and weaponise mourning. Return is reflected in monuments that revise histories to establish new national heroes or rewrite known figures in the national key as a way to establish a link to 'authentic' tradition. In contrast to these three narratives that support the neoliberal-nationalist teleology, I argue that the temporal formation of delay includes monuments that reflect alternative approaches.

But rather than see this as a nationalist/non-nationalist binary, I argue that delay monuments operate as a critical mimesis of Western paradigms of commemoration that produce an entirely different picture of social reality. Before discussing the four temporal formations, I will first unpack two key assumptions underlying my argument: that the temporal realignment of BiH after 1996 has been to fit within the teleology of neoliberalism; and that the temporal narratives established by the monuments symbolically support this teleology.

The Teleology of Neoliberal Transition in BiH

I have previously discussed the way in which the historical condition and social reality in the former Yugoslavia continue to be shaped by Cold War and neo-imperialist divisions: socialist/post-socialist; conflict/post-conflict; Balkan/Europe. The term transition has been one of the key framing devices for the economic and political changes in BiH (and the region of former Yugoslavia in general) in the last two decades (Čvoro 2018). In May 1999, the political and economic representatives of the EU and the IMF set transition as one of the explicit aims for the region's post-communist and post-conflict European integration process, known as the Stabilization and Association Process. These macro policies created a sense of historical inevitability about the 'accession' from centralised economies, conflict and leftovers of colonial empires (Ottoman, Austro-Hungarian and Soviet) towards deregulated markets, stability and European democracy.

I approach transition as an ideology whose interpretative schema is articulated in temporal terms. This ideology has provided the key parameters and framed the political, social and cultural reality in the region in the last two decades. It frames historical events through a series of 'zero hours': the fall of the Berlin Wall in 1989; the dissolution of Yugoslavia and the onset of war in 1991; the Dayton Peace Accord of 1995; and the 'official' start of transition in 1999. It frames the experience of post-socialism as a teleology of normalisation, moving 'away from' the historical error of socialism and 'towards' capitalism and the free market. It articulates the challenges of everyday life in temporal terms – people in difficult situations are painted as being 'left behind' or 'stuck in history'. The temporal schema of this ideology has proclaimed that the 'process' of transition as officially complete (insofar as most of Eastern Europe has been absorbed into the North Atlantic Treaty Organisation (NATO) and coopted into deregulated markets). These kinds of announcements about post-conflict transition are often heard, even though its devastating effects on life in the region – from impoverishment, unemployment, public and private indebtedness, widespread deindustrialisation, political corruption, social degradation, to diminished life expectancy and emigration – show how the narrative of transition of the Yugoslav successor states to a free market and neoliberal democracy has become a euphemism for a 'monumental neo-colonial transformation of this region into a dependent semi-periphery' (Štiks and Horvat 2015: 16). This relates to the understanding of post-socialist transition as a benchmark for progress; BiH as a child of post-socialism that is aspiring to become like the EU. The neoliberal narrative of transition from centralised economies, totalitarianism and conflict towards deregulated markets, stability and European democracy reflects BiH through the prism of belated modernisation. In her analysis of political discourses concerning the accession of the former Yugoslav countries to the EU, Tanja Petrović shows how the narrative of EU integration in the Balkans is presented as the only way for former Yugoslav societies to unburden themselves from historical baggage, from nationalism and other twentieth-century anchors, and join the future-oriented international community (Petrović 2012: 10). However, as Petrović argues, rather than providing an alternative to nationalism(s), transition and EU integration have produced new forms of nationalism.

In this context, to speak of neoliberal temporality in BiH does not only mean referring to accelerationism (the speeding up of production), fragmentation (splintering of the private and social sphere) or techno-managerialist biopolitical utopia (the impact of technology on private and public lives and dissemination of information). It also means to think about the way in which these forms of capital interact with older formations. Miško Šuvaković described this time of the post-socialist transitional state as a hybrid 'monster' made up of parts and traces of almost all historical forms of capitalism: a socially inward realisation of tribal blood-relations into a nineteenth-century romanticist nation-state; an economically assertive-yet-stumbling neoliberal state attempting to fit into contemporary networks of capital; a symbol of the 'second world' where political and economic elites (former communist apparatchiks, former members of the police state-apparatus and *nouveaux riches* tycoons) affect the 'first-phase' accumulation of capital through aggressive (and often illegal) privatisation of the public sphere (Šuvaković 2012: 206–207). These different forms of capital move at different speeds and produce different experiences of time: fantasies about social and class structures of nineteenth-century European national-bourgeoisie collectivism rub up against aspirations towards twenty-first-century global, neoliberal, techno-managerial capital.

What is the role of monuments in a social, political and cultural context so profoundly disjointed in historico-temporal terms? Monuments have traditionally been considered as time-keepers and time-dividers: material markers that divide time into 'before' and 'after' significant events such as wars. Adding another layer of complexity, in BiH, monuments also cut time across ethnic lines to provide three seemingly distinct and mutually exclusive versions of history. In this context, the role of monuments in BiH is to provide conceptions of time's passage that ensure continuity between the present and 'authentic' national history. This not only includes the rewriting of history, where the narrative of a socialist future is excised and replaced with nationalist-neoliberal democracy. This also includes understanding the way in which this reconfiguration of time impacts on understanding property (articulated in Chapter 2 as privatisation of the past), as well as historical accountability and responsibility, and futurity (articulated in Chapter 1 as monumentalisation of the past).

While there are significant overlaps between the temporal categories of leap, loss, return and delay, here I am approaching them separately in order to show through specific examples how each connects to the neoliberal-nationalist nexus. I believe that they provide the way to take a step back from the over-reliance on the 'three nationalisms' narrative in order to see them as variations on the same theme. Also, while the first three categories are dedicated to monuments that can be interpreted as nationalist, the fourth is intended to reflect alternative approaches (usually called civic, or non-nationalist).

Understanding BiH monuments as temporal formations helps us to illustrate how they reflect the broader changes in historical experience and understanding of history. As I argued in the previous chapter, the shift from socialist monuments to nationalist monuments is not simply about replacing one ideology with another. Rather, it is reflective of a changing shape of history and the conception of time's passage.[6] In an immediate sense, socialist history has a shorter timeline, which originates with the emergence of Marxism and class consciousness in the nineteenth century. This means that socialist history is a shallow history with a broad base, intended to reflect transnational solidarity based on ideology. Nationalist history is 'deep' history, which can be projected back in centuries, with a narrow base that is steeped in notions of national and blood kinship. While they both suggest a telos of progress, they nevertheless present entirely different understandings of future-oriented politics: socialist history is based on the linearity of progress towards future utopia, while nationalist history is linked to preservation of the life-cycle of the nation in the current cycle of capital.

Leap

This temporal formation sees the present as connected to the past that predates socialism. The 40 years of socialism are erased or rewritten as undesirable historical and ideological baggage: a rupture in the teleology of the nation. Socialist monuments are the embodiment of this history, and their well-documented systematic destruction and neglect is an attempt to erase this history. But almost just as frequently this heritage is incorporated into the national story. In fact, it is possible to distinguish the way in which attitudes towards monuments reflect the relationship of each group to the memory of World War II. Here we can distinguish between three variations of 'leaps':

Croat leap includes both the erasure of socialist history and its simultaneous transformation as an obstacle to Croat independence. Fascism becomes normalised into a struggle for independence. A high number of World War II monuments have been destroyed in Croat-majority areas as part of the historical revisionism that debased the anti-fascist resistance and rehabilitated the Ustaša regime as part of the narrative of a 'thousand year struggle' for independent Croatia. Examples include the 2013 destruction of a monument 'Tito's Rose' in Široki Brijeg by the local authorities. The act of destruction was framed as a redemption of the dead, because 'Tito's Rose' commemorated fallen Partisan on land underneath which lay Croat victims of those same Partisans. Another example includes the previously discussed dedication of a U-shaped monument in the Modran village to fallen Croat (HVO) soldiers from the 1990s war alongside the 'fallen soldiers from 1941–1947'.

Serb leap absorbs World War II anti-fascist narratives into the greater mythology of Serbian martyrdom. While this sometimes includes the removal of Partisan monuments – such as the 2012 removal of a partisan monument in Bileća and its replacement by a monument to Četniks – in most cases it involves the adaptation of existing Partisan history to fit their narrative. Examples include the monument in Velika Sočanica near Derventa, which mentions fallen 'Serb heroes from the region 1992–1995' on one side and fallen fighters of NOB and 'victims of the fascist terror 1941–1945' on the other. There is a cross on top and a five-point star on the sides. Symbols of different politics and opposed regimes found themselves together on one monument. This fusing of opposing symbolism is best illustrated in the monuments to soldiers from the Army of Republika Srpska (Vojska Republike Srpske VRS) in Brčko, Derventa, Prijedor, Bijeljina and Modriča. All were commissioned by the local authorities and done by Belgrade-based sculptor Miodrag Živković, an award-winning Yugoslav sculptor who designed the well-known NOB monuments in Šumarice, Kragujevac, Tjentište and Kadinjača. Živković easily reverted from celebrated abstract forms to figurative sculptures of Serb martyrs and heavy religious symbolism.

With Bosniaks, in most cases, as socialist monuments do not support the narrative of Bosnia's statehood, they remain largely ignored. There are cases where the victim narrative from NOB is usurped. On a busy intersection on the outskirts of Bosanska Krupa is a *Monument to Amra Sedić*, a 24-year-old 'shahid' (martyr) killed in combat in 1994.

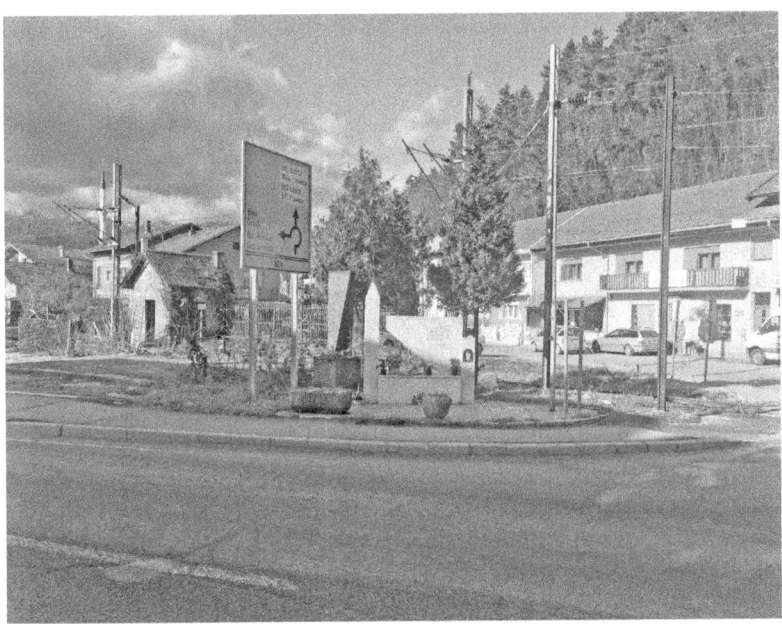

Figure 3.1 Bosanska Krupa, *Monument to Amra Sedić* (Bosanska Krupa, Spomenik Amri Sedić).

The monument is also dedicated to the fallen fighters of the Army of the Republic of Bosnia and Herzegovina (ARBiH) from the local area. While the erection of the monument near a site where Sedić died follows in the established tradition, the positioning of this particular monument is significant. A Sedić monument is placed directly in front of a NOB monument to Lepa Radić, a 17-year-old national hero who was hanged by German SS troops on that site in 1943. The juxtaposition of two monuments and two versions of historical victimology is intentional.[7] The mythology of young fighters sacrificing lives for the greater good of the motherland was one of the main narratives in commemorative World War II practices of Yugoslavia. This trope literally forms the background for the narrative of a young female sacrificing herself while defending BiH. The larger Sedić monument in the shape of BiH blocks the view of the smaller black obelisk in the background. The progressive narrative of female empowerment – a staple of socialist ideology – is starkly contrasted against the heteronormative masculine militarism that permeates the large majority of BiH monuments. Yet, in the case of Sedić, this narrative is put in service of defence. Further, the use of the term 'shahid' (Islamic martyr) repurposes the anti-fascist historical struggle into a fight for BiH independence within the framework of Islam. Anti-fascism and Yugoslavia are useful as a historical platform and framing device to be appropriated.

However, there are also cases where monuments take a distinctively anti-communist position, such as the monument to the organisation 'Young Muslims' at the Kovači cemetery in Sarajevo. This organisation was formed during World War II as an anti-communist pro-Muslim nationalist organisation, which is acknowledged by the inscription dedicated to 'youths killed by the communists in 1945 and 1949'.

The mixture of cynical manipulation and relativisation of NOB by all three sides is strikingly similar – despite some largely cosmetic differences – and reflective of the broader social, political and cultural discourse about the communist past in the last three decades. On the one hand, this discourse transforms the past into a point of difference marked by ambivalence ('our past but not our past'), as evidenced by the widespread destruction and neglect of NOB monuments in BiH. On the other hand, this discourse produces what Buden calls a 'postcommunist subject' characterised by 'free will' that has broken free from the chains of totalitarianism in favour of neoliberal democracy (Buden 2012) and is using the monuments to appropriate its past. Whether this means leaping over a timeline by snipping it out of your historical narrative (Croats), or revising 40 years (Serbs and Bosniaks), the past is not finished or completed but seen as an open process of change.

In an important sense, each regime change is accompanied by a similar rewriting of the past. But even if we accept communist totalitarianism as an accurate representation of the era in BiH, as these narratives would have it, what does the seemingly pathological attachment to discrediting it tell us about the post-communist present in BiH? It connects the neoliberal narrative of the return to 'normality' with the nation-state (or the ethnically pure entity with a patron nation-state) as the frame through which this 'normalization' occurs. We can see evidence of this in official annual ceremonies of important dates, which are fused with NOB histories: in Sarajevo, the celebrations of 'Independence Day' of post-Dayton BiH on March 1 includes official visits to the site of the NOB monument 'Eternal Fire'; and in Banja Luka the 'Day of Republika Srpska' celebrations on January 9 includes laying of wreaths on monuments to the fallen in NOB.

Yet, despite the return to 'normality' through the nationalisation of history, after the fall of socialism, post-socialist revolutionary subjects became historically immature and politically undeveloped obstacles to the introduction of democracy (Buden 2012). The heroes of post-1989 who helped to bring socialism down became a historical-ideological paradox: as the agents that overthrew totalitarianism, and as immature political subjects with a disjointed historical experience. The monument in Obudovac is a good example of this historical disjoint. It commemorates a sequence of wars, citing the number of victims from World War I, World War II, and the 1991–1995 war. It is dedicated to the fallen people of Obudovac from Prota's Uprising (1858) to the present day. The inscription on the monument notes people 'Killed by Ustaše', 'Killed by Četnici' and 'Killed by Partizani', each followed by a list of names. A single monument is dedicated to ideological enemies, all of whom are united after a complex history has been leapt over.

Loss

The temporal narrative of loss is based on self-victimisation in relation to perceived historical struggles against injustice.[8] Monuments that articulate a sense of loss are framed around external threats to the national group. The threats structure and give meaning to the group: if there is no threat, there is no group. In this sense, the symbolism and language of BiH monuments framed around loss is most overtly nationalist. This includes the use of monuments to target and provoke the minority groups in the area by celebrating local 'heroes', or the use of inscriptions that refer to 'fascist aggressors', 'enemy', 'extremists' and 'killers' (UDIK 2017), serving to remind the audience about the threat even at the expense of remembering the victims.

The nationalism of these monuments is framed as an expression of grief. In Chapter 2, I outlined private inat monuments, the kinds of social and familial disputes that they embody and the kinds of temporal narratives that are central to their management and instrumentalisation of death and grief. Here we can expand this definition to include inat monuments done in the name of national groups.[9]

The three-finger salute monument in the village Petkovci near the town of Zvornik is the archetypical inat monument, presenting an aggressive instrumentalisation of death, which is unconstrained by sensitivity to representation of suffering, or historical accuracy.

Located on the side of the main village road, the monument has the form of a black granite hand giving the three-finger Serb nationalist salute. The names, birth and death dates, and photographs of the dead soldiers are distributed across the fingers, and the base of the hand bears the inscription 'People who forget the past have no right to a brighter future'.

In an immediate sense, the 'inat' of the *Petkovci Monument* operates in the form of a highly visible nationalist provocation in a village populated by Serbs and Bosniaks. While the monument is ostensibly about commemorating the dead local soldiers, the nationalist salute in line of sight from the local mosque, and its proximity to sites of mass executions of Bosniaks in the surrounding areas, reframe it as a nationalist instrumentalisation of dead bodies.

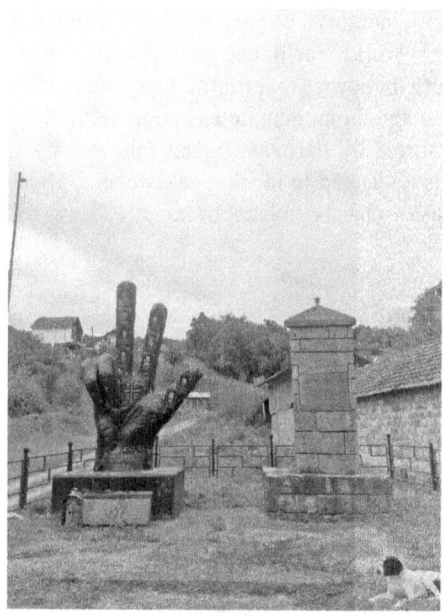

Figure 3.2 Petkovci Monument (Petkovci, Spomenik Palim Borcima).

This was confirmed during my visit to the site, where several passers-by ges-tured back at the monument with the same three-finger salute. This gesture symbolically reanimated the hand and the struggle for a 'brighter future' it represented. Yet, this participatory reanimation of the hand emerging out of the ground also, perhaps unwittingly, recalled the horror film trope of a hand shooting out of the grave. In saluting the dead hand, the locals were engaging in what can be described as zombie nationalism.

The 'inat' of the Pektovci monument also operates through a montage of historical revisionism. The hand is located next to a 1964 monument com-memorating the fallen Partisan fighters from World War II bearing the dedi-cation to all who gave their lives for 'freedom and brotherhood and unity of our people'. The three-fingered hand manipulates the anti-fascist struggle into a Serb struggle for independence. But it does so through a striking cogni-tive leap: the inscription on the hand instructs its 'people' (the Serbs) to never forget history, except perhaps when it does not fit the nationalist narrative, such as the history of trans-national solidarity commemorated by the Partisan monument located beside it. In this sense, the 'brighter future' enunciated by the Pektovci monument aligns with the 'light at the end of the tunnel' from the banner displayed on the 9th January highway I discussed in Chapter 1.[10]

The two constructions close the temporal loop of negating the socialist past in order to clean the slate for the inevitability of the nationalist-neoliberal present.

The strategy of building an inat monument to oppose or negate an existing one can also operate on a shorter historical cycle, where monuments are constructed in relation to events from the 1990s and in reaction to another monument at the same site. This is evident in what can be termed as 'standoff monuments' in the town centres of Jajce and Brčko. In both cases, monuments to fallen 'liberators' – Croat and Bosniak fighters in Jajce, and Croat, Bosniak and Serb fighters in Brčko – stand in close proximity of monuments to other 'liberators', which fought against each other during the war. In Jajce, the two monuments are literally across the road from each other. Both were built on private land, again confirming the significance of privatisation in the construction of monuments: the Croat monument was built on the site of a destroyed house, which was donated by the owner and financed by the HVO veteran's association, and the ARBiH monument was built on land owned by the local mosque (the monument is in the front yard of the mosque).

Monumental stand-offs are also present in depopulated areas, such as the monument to Bosniak fighters on the side of gravel road in the small village Ledići near Trnovo. Across the road, on private property, there is a monument to civilian Serb victims from the village. These two opposing memories face each other, engaging in a monumental stand-off on an empty, remote gravel road. The claim of ownership over territory through the monument appears utterly redundant in the context of an abandoned village.

This is also evident in Trnopolje, a small village near Prijedor, where a large monument was erected there in honour of fallen fighters. The inscription on the monument reads: 'To soldiers who built their lives into the foundations of Republic of Srpska'. It is accompanied by patriotic verses by Petar Kočić and Taras Shevchenko, the latter in Ukrainian. The monument is the shape of an eagle made out of concrete. It is situated at the site of what used to be a camp for non-Serbs at the beginning of the war, where women, children and the elderly were interned, where 23,000 people had been imprisoned and where abuse and rape were commonplace. The building of the former camp still stands, less than ten meters away from the monument and no indication that it used to be a camp. Local Serb officials still deny that it was a camp, claiming that it was a 'collection centre' for refugees.

When I visited the village in late 2018, it was half-deserted, with poorly kept houses everywhere. The monument itself was in poor condition, with traces of weather damage.

The panel with the Shevchenko poem was missing, and weeds were growing around the monument. Wilting flower wraiths lay at the base. The monument was showing signs of premature ageing, as if to reinforce that

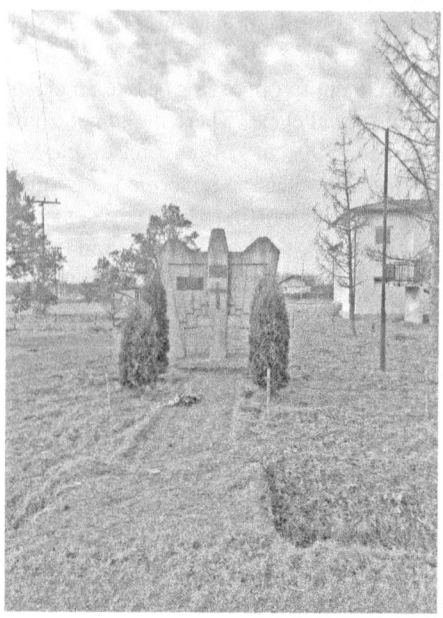

Figure 3.3 Prijedor, *Monument to the Fallen Republika Srpska Fighters from Trnopolje* (Prijedor, Spomen-obilježje palim borcima RS iz Trnopolja).

it referred to a time that was a necessary step in the transitional road to the present. It resembled the Modran village monument, which I discussed in Chapter 1. However, in contrast to Modran, which was a majority Croat village, Petkovci was divided between Serbs and Bosniaks. A few streets away were monuments erected to the fallen Bosniaks. Monuments were being used to claim symbolic ownership of territories that have been abandoned.

Inat monuments can also refuse to mark the site of violence. While such denial is clearly linked to nationalist politics, it is also important to understand the way in which this denial enables the influx of global capital in the region. This is best illustrated through the example of an Omarska mine located a few kilometres away from Trnopolje. The buildings at Omarska were used as a camp by Bosnian Serbs from May–August 1992.[11] With over 3000 Bosniaks and Croats imprisoned, over 700 killed and thousands still missing, this camp became the symbol of systematic cruelty. No form of commemoration exists on the site despite repeated calls by locals and NGOs, and commercial mining operations have resumed after the mine was purchased in 2004 by ArcelorMittal, one of the world's largest steel producers.

In this sense, the entire site represents an inat monument because it stands as a reminder of the refusal to acknowledge the suffering of non-Serbs in the area. But crucially, this refusal is not only linked to nationalist politics, but also their proximity to the influx of global capital into the region. There are two ways in which this story links the flow of global capital and genocide in the region. First, the site has been used as the location for Srdjan Dragojević's film 'St George Slays the Dragon' (2009). This prompted Pavle Levi to write an essay (Levi 2009) outlining the connection between a site of systemic ethnic cleansing used to establish Republika Srpska, that site being used for filming a Serb epic historical war movie, and that site being reactivated for profit extraction by the ArcelorMittal Orbit corporation.[12] Second, iron ore and profits extracted from Omarska have been used by ArcelorMittal Orbit to manufacture London's Olympic tower.[13] These two ways illustrate the complex spatio-temporal nexus of inat monuments and neoliberalism. Spatially, they connect the camp in Omarska, the Olympic Tower in London and a global corporation based in India. Temporally, they connect Serb World War I (movie), Socialism (state-owned mine), colonialism (land dispossession and exploitation of people in India) and neoliberalism (profit extraction and investment across the world).

We can add another historico-temporal layer to the story. London's Olympic Tower was inspired by Vladimir Tatlin's design for the *Monument to the Third International* (1919–1920), an unrealised utopian project intended to celebrate the spirit of the Soviet Revolution. Tatlin's structure has served as an inspiration for numerous projects because it has become an iconic image of revolutionary utopia.[14] Its referencing by the London Olympic Tower marks a co-option of revolutionary art in the service of celebrating global capital. But there is yet another sense of historical repetition at play. London's Olympic Tower has been plagued with structural problems since its opening, echoing the unrealised Tatlin's project. The utopian monument to (failed) revolution becomes the failed monument to the nexus of neo-colonial global capital and genocide.

The connection of inat monuments to neoliberalism is not only evident through land and resource privatisation, but also in the way in which their construction is often strategically connected to political and media cycles. It is important to remember that the appearance of each inat monument has been accompanied by a media event of outrage (UDIK 2018) that recalls the injustices and enables the different sides to recount its version of history. This clearly indicates that the construction is a calculated move to provoke as well as to ensure high media visibility and the presence of debates. The saturation of the media sphere by such stories increases in frequency and intensity in election years, indicating that loss and grief are instrumentalised and linked to election cycles.

Return

While the temporal narrative of loss is based on identifying external threats to national identity, monuments based around the narrative of return represent a sense of 're-emergence' of national identity based around nineteenth-century romanticist notions of organic community: national roots, constitutive visions of tradition, blood bonds and kinship. BiH monuments framed around the idea of return celebrate national 'heroes' with no distinction between which wars or which sides of that conflict are being commemorated. Soldiers that fought in World War I, World War II and the 1990s; soldiers that fought with the partisans, with nationalist militias, fascist collaborators, victims of communist executions all get conflated on single structures in historical montages. But rather than attempts to present universal messages or take an internationalist approach, these montages use the symbolic capital of ideologies and identities to mark the return of the national group.

This is evident in monuments built by all three main ethnic groups in BiH. The monument in the Obudovac village near Šamac is dedicated to 'all fallen Serbs' (including soldiers from wars in the nineteenth century to the 1990s who fought on opposite sides) who fought to 'preserve the homeland, their homes and the Orthodox faith'; and a monument near Modriča that commemorates a battle from 1858, World War II Četnik units and Serbs fallen in a battle from 1992. Croat examples include the monument in Donji Crnač near Široki Brijeg, which combines the šahovnica, Catholic cross, symbols of the Independent State of Croatia (Nezavisna Država Hrvatska NDH) (shaped as the letter 'V' which was sometimes used by Ustase as a substitute for 'U') and a monument in Dračevo near Čapljina, which commemorates a 1875 Croat uprising against 'Turkish and Serb oppression on Croat land'. Monuments at Radmilje village near Stolac and Rasno village near Široki Brijeg are dedicated to 'Croats who fell fighting for the motherland' with a special emphasis on the events at Bleiburg. They are both monuments dedicated to victims of communists. In the case of Bosniaks, this is evident in the monument to Huska Miljković in Velika Kladuša, a World War II leader of Muslim Militia who collaborated with the Germans and Ustase only to place himself under partisan command in 1944 and die under suspicious circumstances. He is celebrated as one of the greatest Bosniak heroes.

The temporal formation of return relates to neoliberalism through the creation of what I have previously described as halfway tradition (Čvoro 2018). In her analysis of political discourses concerning the accession of the former Yugoslav countries to the EU, Tanja Petrović shows how the narrative of EU integration in the Balkans is presented as the only way for former Yugoslav societies to unburden themselves from historical baggage, from nationalism and other twentieth-century anchors, and join the future-oriented international community. However, rather than providing an alternative to nationalism(s), transition and EU integration have produced new forms of nationalism: reconfiguring historical timelines to provide continuity between the present and the 'authentic' national history through reburials of dead bodies; exhibiting cultural idiosyncrasies through the international art circuit; 'traditionalizing' societies through giving traditional names to newborn children and promoting consumption of traditional food, music, arts and crafts (Malesević 2005).

Halfway tradition is the accidental consequence of the production of the national past. Sociologist Ildiko Erdei, in her account of subjectivities in post-socialism and the formation of the halfway position, argues that the transition from socialism to capitalism is underpinned by an assumption that it will also involve a change from socialist subjects to capitalist subjects (Erdei 2011: 276). Yet once decoupled from a socialist way of life – such as dependence on the state for social support, belief in a better tomorrow, cynical distance towards the system and opposition to Western values – the subjects of post-socialism never successfully transitioned into neoliberal subjects and remained caught in-between, even taking on the 'worst' parts from both systems: corruption from old socialist networks and cynical opportunism and exploitation from neoliberalism.

So who are the halfway heroes returning through BiH monuments? In addition to the historical figures in the above examples, return monuments also include more recent figures, such as the monument to indicted war criminal Ratko Mladić in his birthplace Kalinovik, monuments to Franjo Tuđman (first president to independent Croatia and father of contemporary Croat nationalism) (2003) and Gojko Šušak (Croat defence minister in the 1990s) (2008) in Široki Brijeg. They are halfway heroes because they are all communist converts who opportunistically turned to nationalism as a mobiliser, and who achieved their positions of power through a variety of criminal activities that include genocide, nepotism, war and post-war looting. In short, they are the success stories of genocidal neoliberal dispossession. Their commitment to nationalism – celebrated by monuments dedicated to them and their struggle for the nation – obscures the accumulation by dispossession that has been intrinsic to the regimes they represent. And it is precisely this dispossession in the guise of national populist authoritarianism that connects them to the formation of the nineteenth-century nation-state.

Delay

From the discussion thus far, it would appear that the large majority of the monuments built in BiH since 1996 exist firmly within the nationalist framework. The following section outlines the Bruce Lee monument in Mostar, and *Monument to the International Community* and *Under This Stone There Is a Monument to the Victims of War and Cold War* in Sarajevo as projects that are critical of this framework, or attempt to move beyond it. I argue that these projects should be seen as forms of temporal delay in relation to the neoliberal understanding of the centre-periphery relation between BiH and EU. These monuments critically reflect the assumption that post-socialist and post-conflict states such as BiH can never match their counterparts in the 'developed world' and end up being a delayed mimesis (of a postmodernist mimesis) of Western culture. I argue that delay monuments use mimesis as a critical tool to unpack this centre-periphery relationship.

The critical agency of these monuments can be traced by their origin in the project *De/construction of Monument* (2004–2007), which included a series of panel discussions, lectures and seminars, artistic presentations, exhibitions and interventions in public space. Led by curator Dunja Blažević, hosted by the Center for Contemporary Art Sarajevo and sponsored by international organisations, the project culminated in a public competition for a 'new monument' in BiH, which included the installation of the top designs in Sarajevo and Mostar (SCCA 2007). The fact that monuments critical of nationalism emerged out of an artistic project and competition seemingly confirms that artists have a greater sense of autonomy and critical agency towards BiH. In contrast to the majority of other monuments in BiH, the three projects discussed here take a critical position towards nationalism based in mimicry. Bruce Lee engages with popular culture and *Monument to the International Community* reflects on the tropes of Western humanitarianism.

However, the trajectory of these monuments following their unveiling also takes on the characteristics of mimicry (through repetition), albeit in unexpected ways. Through destruction, vandalism and reconstruction, these monuments take on lives beyond what the artists originally intended. In discussing unexpected forms of delay and mimicry, I will return to the question of these monuments as the default counter-monuments in BiH.

I have previously written about the events surrounding the November 2005 unveiling of the Bruce Lee monument in Mostar (Čvoro 2014). Spearheaded by the non-governmental organisation, Mostar Urban Movement, the life-sized monument of Lee was intended as a symbol of solidarity and fighting against ethnic divisions in the community. On the night the monument opened, a group of teenagers spray painted the statue, stole Lee's nunchucks and left the site littered with bottles. The statue was moved to a warehouse, with only the pedestal remaining to bear the inscription: 'To Bruce Lee, your Mostar'. I argued that the vandalising of the Bruce Lee statue was a repetition of the destruction of the sixteenth-century Stari Most (Old Bridge) 13 years earlier on 9 November 1993.[15] Stari Most was the symbol of Mostar's history and cultural diversity (the city's name translates as 'the bridge keeper') and its destruction symbolised the civic destruction of the multiethnic and cosmopolitan community in the Yugoslav wars of the 1990s. Although the vandalising of the Bruce Lee statue was a repetition of the destruction of the bridge, I argued that the difference in the magnitude and scale of the destruction – between a premeditated destruction of an iconic sixteenth-century bridge symbolic of both a multiethnic town and a multiethnic country, and the drunken vandalising of a bronze statue of a popular culture icon – recalled Marx's paraphrase of Hegel that history happens twice – the first time as tragedy and the second time as farce.

Here we can add another chapter to this story. Bruce Lee was returned to Mostar's central park in 2013 and the return is once again repeating the history of Stari Most.

Stari Most was reopened in 2004 with much fanfare and celebration of how the reconstruction bridged divides. While it was meant to symbolise the reunification of the divided city, the unification never eventuated, and Mostar continues to be a city-symbol of the inherent divisions and systemic political dysfunction in BiH. Through its destruction and reconstruction, Stari Most shifted from being an 'unintentional monument' to a multiethnic city to becoming a top-down 'staged reconciliation' disconnected from the realities of the divided city (Forde 2016: 468). In this sense, the identification of Stari Most with the reconciliation aligns the process of post-conflict transition with the physical restoration.[16]

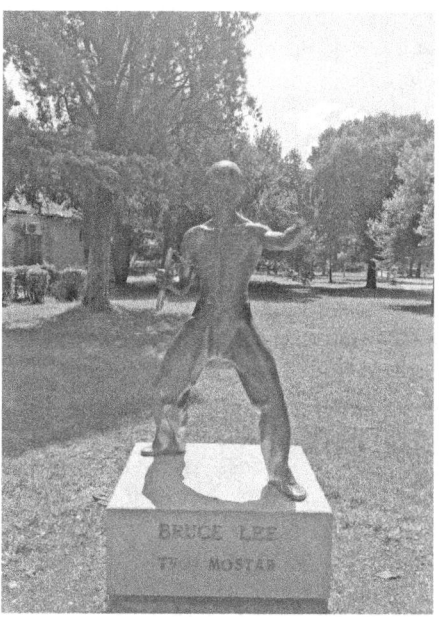

Figure 3.4 Bruce Lee Statue, Mostar.

The Bruce Lee monument was returned to the city park in 2013, with little fanfare and media commentary, and no further acts of vandalism. Seemingly, the symbol of reconciliation was physically restored only to be consigned to obsolescence and invisibility, except for serving as a popular selfie spot. But the Bruce Lee monument returning has been overshadowed by the very public political shift of its two originators Nino Raspudić and Veselin Gatalo, who were collaborating under the name of Mostar Urban Movement. In the years since the original removal of the statue, they have both become staunch nationalists: Raspudić a mouthpiece for Croat nationalism in BiH, and Gatalo a staple on regime-supporting Serb nationalist television. They claim to still remain as good friends, proving two cliches: that yesterdays radicals are tomorrows conservatives; and that different nationalisms are perfectly compatible.

Bruce Lee mimics the mimicry of Stari Most as a symbol of reconciliation. Just as Stari Most becomes an anti-monument to Mostar, Bruce Lee has become the reverse of what it was intended to be. The two structures are entwined as historical and temporal markers of staged reconciliation and its utopian symbols.

This sense of the present as the ironic end of utopia is also the subject of Nebojša Šerić Šoba's sculptural work *Monument to the International Community* (2007).

Another of the winning designs to emerge from *De/construction of Monument*, and erected in central Sarajevo on the fifteenth anniversary of the start of the Bosnian war, the work is a giant can of spam. The work features the can on a pedestal with the inscription 'from the grateful citizens of Sarajevo'. The work is a powerful indictment of the role of the international community in the war. It ridicules 'both the UN's humanitarian assistance during the war, and the internationally influenced project of post-war commemoration' (Sheftel 2011: 157). It captures the inadequacy and the belatedness of the international community's response to the atrocities in Bosnia, by symbolising international humanitarianism as an unappetising can of spam given to the starving population of Sarajevo during the war, despite often being past its expiry date. *Monument to the International Community* uses the familiar scale, placement and aesthetic of monuments. The humanitarian aid was as late as international intervention in BiH; and the gratitude of the citizens of Sarajevo is a cynical one: thanking the international community for their inaction which held to set BiH back by decades. The additional twist on the temporal delay of this monument is provided by the multiple vandalisms of the structure and the lack of general upkeep. This has even led to demands by the artist that the monument is removed and taken to another country that would appreciate it. Seemingly, the ungrateful public has started engaging with the monument as the proxy for the international community.

The fates of Bruce Lee and *Monument to the International Community* need to be understood in the context of their frequent invocation as

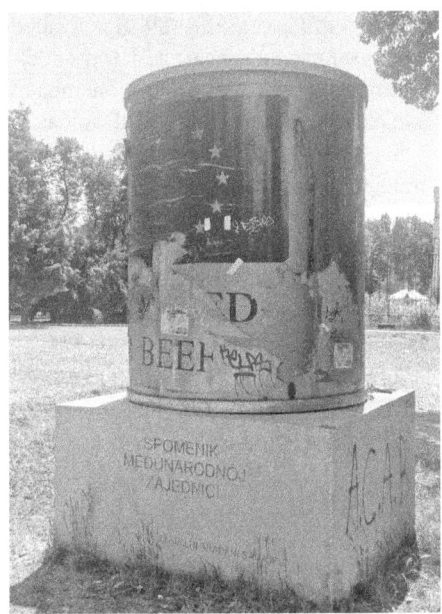

Figure 3.5 Nebojša Šerić Šoba, *Monument to the International Community for the Grateful Citizens of Sarajevo* (2007).

counter-monuments in BiH. They both attest to the lack of consensus in the experience of the audience, and act as reminders about the failed attempts to construct monuments in BiH. They function as reminders of the ongoing neglect and misunderstanding of BiH, including the use of counter-monuments as an interpretative framework.

The burden of commemoration in BiH underpins the winning work of the 'New Monument' competition as part of *De/construction of Monument.* Braco Dimitrijević's *Under This Stone There Is a Monument to the Victims of War and Cold War* is a large stone block (150x150x300 cm), engraved with the title text on four sides in four languages (English, German, BHS and French). It is located next to the building of the former Museum of the Revolution, that was established in 1945 and converted into the Historical Museum of Bosnia and Herzegovina in 1993.

The work is a direct reference to Esther Shalev-Gerz and Jochen Gerz's *Monument Against Fascism* – the archetypal 'counter-monument'. It brings our discussion back to the question of using counter-monumentality as the interpretative framework for BiH monuments, discussed in Chapter 1. Dimitrijević's use of this aesthetic is an intentional delayed mimesis. This is suggested through his use of language, materiality and location of the monument. The monument is seemingly commemorating the Cold War: a conflict assumed as over following the 'end of history' in 1989. It is located outside of an institution that has been systematically neglected and underfunded. And it uses a format that is firmly rooted in outdated monumental minimalism. Yet, this mimesis of obsolescence, this intentional archaism reframes the historical constellation that make up the context of the monument. Dimitrijević's mimesis is a strategic form of historico-temporal self-colonisation in which external solutions are always better than local ones. In Dimitrijević's work, the recent history of BiH is filled by poorly timed decisions: the international intervention to stop the war in BiH arrived too late and too little; the internationally mandated reconciliation was early and largely staged; but the temporal displacement of both events was forced onto BiH as the historical and temporal framework. In this context, using counter-monumentality is once again moving the dialogue backwards by insisting on an outdated and inappropriate term to understand a complex historical situation.

***

Monuments are said to divide and join time: they divide time into 'before' and 'after' something happened; they join time by bringing particular histories into the present. If this temporal imperative is at the core of all monument construction, then the recent hyper-production of monuments in BiH is a signal that there is much historical editing to justify the rule of nationalists in the present. But monuments are also representative of particular shapes of time: the linearity of progress, the repetition of the past and the cycle of violence. My aim in this chapter has been to show that the four narratives that underpin BiH post-conflict monuments reflect variations on transition as a historical conjuncture. This approach treats transition as a geopolitical construction of time, and monuments as cultural objects operating within and casting light on this historical conjuncture. So, what is this geopolitical construction of time? It is the combination of the sense of collective entrapment in the BiH meantime with exhortations to move on the road to Europe political maturity. My approach to monuments as temporal formations of neoliberalism has attempted to show that nationalism, rather than the cause for the current predicament of BiH, should be seen as a symptom of neoliberal decimation of society. It is my hope that seeing monuments in this way may be the first step in forging a sense of solidarity that transcends national divides.

Notes

1 One notable exception to this rule is the Memorial Centre Srebrenica – Potočari, whose construction was approved by the High Representative for BiH and funded internationally.

2 Most reports on the monuments indicate the absence of a commissioned artist, suggesting that they were most likely produced by local stonemasons who make gravestones.

3 The most recent example is the naming of a student accommodation building in Pale after Radovan Karadžić.

4 There are other examples, such as the 2016 unveiling of a monument in Vareš to all victims of war, featuring no religious inscriptions and the official emblem of BiH, with an inscription 'pay respects in your own way'. Despite the seemingly unifying message of the monument, after completion the local Croat party HDZ removed it shortly after winning the local seat in elections.

5 I draw on Šuvaković's (2012) account to articulate the four temporal formations. For a full development of these four formations, see Čvoro (2018).

6 The following paragraph draws on Verdery's (1999) articulation of the historical shift between communism and nationalism in Eastern Europe.

7 It is worth mentioning that less than a kilometre away in the town centre is a large commemorative fountain dedicated to all local fighters.

8 Here I am relying on Žižek's account of nationalism in the former Yugoslavia. Žižek uses Lacan to argue that nationalism is centred around imagined theft of enjoyment that was never possessed in the first place. See (Žižek 1993: 203)

9 The term 'inat monuments' (inat spomenici) has often been used in BiH media to describe intentionally provocative and overtly nationalist monuments.

10 This alignment is even more apparent in Bosnian-Serbo-Croatian. 'Svijetlija budućnost' from the monument is 'svijetlo na kraju tunela' from the highway.

11 It is important to note that Omarska, while most blatant, is certainly not the only case of intentional refusal to mark the site of suffering by others. Other examples include Kazani, near Sarajevo, a location where a number of Serb civilians were executed during the Sarajevo siege and Silos camp near Tarčin, which was under the control of ARBiH. On the denial of these crimes, see Moll 2015.

12 Levi's essay in turn triggered the formation of the artistic group 'Three Faces of Omarska'.

13 The Three Faces of Omarska group carried out a project in response called 'a memorial in exile' where they reclaimed the Olympic Orbit.

14 In addition to the structural unfeasibility of Tatlin's idea, the gigantic amount of steel required for the structure was not available in bankrupt post-revolutionary Russia.

15 In an additional level of historical irony 9 November 1989 was the date when the government of Eastern Germany announced that its citizens could cross into Western Germany. This date is often considered to be the start of the fall of the Berlin Wall.

16 Through the completion of the reconstruction, Stari Most and the surrounding area Stari Grad became an internationally certified UNESCO World Heritage Site and was regarded as a 'symbol of reconciliation'.

References

Buden, B. (2012) *Zona Prelaska: O Kraju Postkomunizma*. Beograd: Fabrika Knjiga.

Čvoro, U. (2014) *Turbo-Folk Music and Cultural Representations of National Identity in Former Yugoslavia*. London: Ashgate.

Čvoro, U. (2018) *Transitional Aesthetics: Contemporary Art at the Edge of Europe*. London: Bloomsbury.

Erdei, I. (2011) "Rocky Made In Serbia": Globalne Ikone. In Prica, I. and Skokić, T. (eds) *Horror Porno Ennui: Kulture Prakse Postsocijalizma*. Zagreb: Biblioteka Nova Etnografija, pp. 273–298.

Forde, S. (2016) The Bridge on the Neretva: Stari Most as a Stage of Memory in Post-Conflict Mostar, Bosnia–Herzegovina. *Cooperation and Conflict*, 51(4): 467–483.

Kappler, S. (2017) Sarajevo's Ambivalent Memoryscape: Spatial Stories of Peace and Conflict. *Memory Studies*, 10(2): 130–143.

Kurto, N. (2006) Memory of the Dying City. In Junuzović, Azra (ed) *Sarajevo Roses: Towards Politics of Remembering*. Sarajevo: Armis Print i Udruženje za zaštitu tekovina borbe za Bosnu I Hercegovinu, pp. 147–150.

Levi, P. (2009) Kapo iz Omarske. *Beton* No 68. Available at: http://www.elektrobeton. net/strafta/kapo-iz-omarske/ (accessed 22 October 2018).

Malesević, M. (2005) Tradicija u Tranziciji: U Potrazi za "Još Starijim i Lepšim" Identitetom. In Radojičič, Dragana (ed) *Etnologija i Antropologija: Stanje I Perspektive*. Beograd: Zbornik Etnografskog Institut SANU, Volume 21, pp. 219–234.

Moll, N. (2015) *Sarajevska najpoznatija javna tajna, Suočavanje sa Cacom, Kazanima i zločinima počinjenim nad Srbima u opkoljenom Sarajevu od rata do 2015*. Sarajevo: Friedrich Ebert Foundation BiH.

Petrović, T. (2012) *Yuropa: Jugoslovensko Nasledje I Politike Buducnosti u Postjugoslovenskim Drustvima*. Beograd: Fabrika Knjiga.

Ristić, M. (2018) *Architecture, Urban Space and War: The Destruction and Reconstruction of Sarajevo*. London: Palgrave Macmillan.

SCCA (2007) *De/construction of Monument*. Available at: http://scca.ba/scca-proje cts/deconstruction-of-monument/ (accessed 6 November 2018).

Sheftel, A. (2011) Monument to the International Community, from the Grateful Citizens of Sarajevo: Dark Humour as Counter-memory in Post-conflict Bosnia-Herzegovina. *Memory Studies*, 5(2): 145–164.

Štiks, I. and Horvat, S. (2015) Introduction: Radical Politics in the Desert of Transition. In Štiks, I. and Horvat, S. (eds) *Welcome to the Desert of Post-Socialism*. London: Verso, pp. 1–20.

Šuvaković, M. (2012) *Umetnost I Politika: Savremena Estetika, Filozofija, Teorija I Umetnost u Vremenu Globalne Tranzicije*. Beograd: Savremeni Glasnik.

UDIK (2017) *The Association for Social Research and Communications Central Register of Monuments*. Sarajevo: UDIK.

UDIK (2018) *Spomenici I Politike Sjećanja U BiH I Republci Hrvatskoj: Kontroverze*. Sarajevo: UDIK.

Verdery, K. (1999) *The Political Lives of Dead Bodies*. New York: Columbia University Press.

Žižek, S. (1993) *Tarrying With the Negative*. London: Verso.

Afterword

When speaking to a group of university students in Banja Luka in 2018, I was struck by their articulation of how the recent history of BiH related to their personal experience. After I explained that I was researching BiH postwar monuments, most of the students were surprised that such monuments existed. They informed me that the 1990s war was not covered in school curriculum, and that their parents hardly ever spoke to them about this period. They said that most of what they know about the period came from relatives who were willing to speak about it (usually from a nationalist perspective) and from the media (usually wrapped in a political spin). While they actively tried to ignore the nationalism inherent in such public and private conversations, at the same time they felt that their whole lives have been ruled and determined by nationalist politics, against their wishes.

I start here by reflecting on the relation of young people to monuments in BiH because they are (presumably) the intended audience. But rather than inspiring them or forging a sense of historical consciousness, the monuments had the opposite effect on young people of BiH, seemingly confirming the often-repeated trope that there is nothing as invisible as a public monument (Musil 1987). But even if the monuments were invisible to young people and indeed large numbers of the population, they nevertheless framed the perception of BiH in the public sphere in almost exclusively nationalist terms. This nationalist dispossession of space and time felt like a total and overwhelming monopolisation of public and private historical experience. Within contemporary BiH, people are seemingly only able to situate themselves in terms of nationalist histories, or in opposition to them. There is no alternative.

So where does this leave BiH monuments? At the time of this writing, there is very little to indicate that the rate of monument construction is going to decrease. At a time when production of BiH is in rapid decline – with factories closing and skilled labour leaving the country in thousands – monument construction is on the rise. In what seems like a weekly occurrence, there are new reports of monuments being constructed, new controversies over insensitive and offensive commemorations, or another outrage over war criminals or fascist collaborators being celebrated. And in most of these cases, while the monuments are the initiative of individuals or interest groups, the authorities are doing little to prevent, and often a lot to enable their construction.

The only construction that is seemingly happening at even greater speed and intensity than monuments in BiH is the construction of neoliberal infrastructure. As young people are leaving, the country itself is getting more half-empty shopping centres and nationalist monuments. This is the nationalist-neoliberal nexus: parallel economies of construction each determined by its capital, both of which define the temporal axis of the present. Nationalist rhetoric defining the unfinished history usurping the present, and neoliberal infrastructure defining the movement towards the future of capital. This nexus defines the temporal directionality of 'Balkan nationalism' in the process of 'becoming Europe' by being integrated, or dissolved, into the invisible global infrastructure of capitalist production.

Importantly, this is not to say that all individually initiated monuments in BiH are nationalist. In fact, there are several cases where people or organisations showed initiative (and entrepreneurialism) in order to secure funds for construction of monuments. In November 2019, NGO UDIK announced a public competition for a monument to the killed civilians at Kazani near Sarajevo. This monument is intended to serve as a monument to all civilian casualties in BiH. UDIK has been instrumental in raising public awareness in BiH over the normative politics of commemoration, and behind a number of initiatives that attempt to move the conversation beyond nationalism, revisionism and neo-fascism.

But these acts of solidarity also happen through individual initiatives. In August 2018, a memorial plaque was erected on the gate of an Orthodox cemetery near Konjic. The small plaque was positioned on the left-hand side of the entrance gate to the cemetery. It featured an engraved image of two young boys embracing and walking away with their backs turned to us. Beneath, the text reads 'Gate raised in memory of Golubović Petar 7 years and Pavle 5 years by Anis Kosovac' (Radio Sarajevo 2018). Kosovac is a local living nearby who raised the funds for the plaque and renovation of the gate to the old cemetery after years of inactivity from the local council. The plaque commemorates a horrific event from July 1992, when the two boys and their parents were forcibly removed from their flat by members of Konjic Special Police Forces and shot in nearby woods.

These examples of individual acts of empathy suggest that the people of BiH are not entirely duped by the nationalist rhetoric. Mass protests in 2014 across the country against political nepotism and corruption, along with protests calling for justice for David and Dženan, ultimately failed to topple the political elite, but identified power and corruption outside of the nationalist rhetoric. These examples also illustrate that the political apparatus in BiH is entirely dependent on nationalism for its validation. This success has been in large part because it addresses the individual and the core subject of capitalism – the fulfillment of national independence is the celebration of the individual. Thus, the hyper-production of monuments in a race to commemorate and monumentalise the recent past in BiH is underpinned by the desire to forget the fundamental absence of collectivity. Despite political claims about fulfillments of national 'dreams of independence', the divided memory space in BiH shows us that there are no winners after the 1990s, and the first step outside of the nationalist-neoliberal nexus may be in making that admission.

The work of the artist Mladen Miljanović is an exemplary attempt to search for the meaning of collectivism in monuments beyond nationalism. His body of work exhibited in Banja Luka in late 2019 under the title *Aperta Fenestra* reimagines monuments by focusing on their lived and social function. Miljanović's repurposing of monuments – whether recreating them as participatory events with marginalised social groups such as war veterans, planting them into manure or physically carrying their weight – intervenes into the politically charged BiH monumental free market in which the ability to commemorate is not based on ethical, moral or aesthetic considerations, but on access to resources and proximity to political power. But if Miljanović's practice is framed by the political complexities and absurdities of his local context, he is equally interested in the significance of citing modernist monuments in that context. He is aware that the current proliferation of monuments in BiH exists in the historical shadow of modernism monuments in Yugoslavia, which continue to play central roles in the simultaneous destruction and revision of a shared past and the establishment of national histories. His body of work is the first systematic attempt to address these questions, more than a decade after the *De/construction of Monument* project. While it warrants a more detailed analysis in an international context – which is beyond the scope of this book – it is significant to mention here as a way to question the meaning and function of monuments at a time of historical amnesia, revisionism and normalisation of fascism.

On the one hand, this includes the continuing presence of Yugoslavia as a historical and political reference, despite its persistent discrediting by the political and nationalist elites over the last three decades. This discrediting spans: demonisation of Yugoslav socialist system as corrupt, undemocratic and self-destructive; trivialisation of the lived memory of Yugoslavia as nostalgic and naïve; destruction of socialist monuments; and rehabilitation of local World War II fascists and their collaborators. On the other hand, this also includes the relation of monuments to extreme relativism that fuses shameless historical cherry picking and toxic genocide denial and revisionism with access to political power. Historical experience is relativised to the point where it functions like predatory capital: it punctures and permeates all aspects of the social sphere of everyday life, it relies on corruption and it breeds self-interest. Importantly, in focusing on BiH, my intention has not been to argue its exceptionalism. In fact, one of the key problems of approaching BiH monuments has been the distinct sense of exoticisation from local and international commentators. Rather, I believe that the case of memorial culture in BiH not only mirrors but anticipates the future of Europe, much like the dissolution of Yugoslavia in the early 1990s anticipated many of the current events in Europe. Understanding the current memorial culture in BiH beyond the identitarian nationalist matrix is key to understanding its connection to neoliberalism: that nationalism is not a reaction to neoliberalism but its enabler. In addition, a critique of conservative, religious, patriarchal and nationalist hegemony of the post-Yugoslav societies needs to be a critique of the neoliberal capitalist transformation that accompanied and enabled that transformation.

In this context, BiH monuments should not only be seen as studies of identity constructions. They should be seen as identity constructions that are steeped in particular constructions of history and experiences of time. I have attempted to draw attention to the way in which these constructions are determined by retroactively. Temporal nationalist constructions project a view that BiH's last few centuries have been shaped by little more than struggles between national groups for independence and freedom, and that a weaponised culture of commemoration is only the latest phase of this struggle.

BiH here appears as a particular history (of ethnic hatred) and a historical category (unstable periphery). In this history, if BiH in the 1990s was always about the national question and ethnic conflict, BiH in the second decade of the twenty-first century is about the re-introduction of capital and deregulation. In this historical category, solidarity is being replaced by the historical determinism of political divisions, difficult historical legacies and religious differences. And the population is being forced to live in what seems like a repetition of its colonial past: whether it is the ethnoconfessional division inherited from the Ottoman rule, the romanticist nationalism of the Habsburg empire or reheated Cold War alliances. But the one constant is the logic of economic exploitation by the elites. This is the spectre that is haunting the commemorative space of BiH, and this could be the uniting driver, just like it was in people demanding for justice for David, Dženan and all the children of BiH.

References

Musil, R. (1987) Monuments. In *Posthumous Papers of a Living Author*, translated by Peter Wortsman. Hygiene Col, pp. 64–68.

Radio Sarajevo (2018) Available at: https://www.radiosarajevo.ba/metromahala/lica/anis-kunovac-ja-sam-samo-ostao-normalan-covjek/311939 (accessed 11 September 2018).

Index

For Product Safety Concerns and Information please contact our EU
representative GPSR@taylorandfrancis.com
Taylor & Francis Verlag GmbH, Kaufingerstraße 24, 80331 München, Germany

www.ingramcontent.com/pod-product-compliance
Lightning Source LLC
Chambersburg PA
CBHW061151180526
45170CB00002B/721